ALL

IN

For Those in Search of Something More

Written By Adam Palmer

Edited by Stacy Padula

Briley & Baxter Publications | Plymouth, Massachusetts

ISBN: 9781954819139

Book Design: Stacy O'Halloran
Cover Design: Mackenzie Wells

Dedication

To my King, Savior, and best friend, Jesus; I don't know why you would ever want anything to do with me, but for some unknown reason, you love me more than I could ever imagine.

To My Little Bunny Rabbit. I'm truly grateful for the way you have always supported me, no matter what…. I know it hasn't always been easy being married to a guy like me, but I hope that it's been worth it.

To our children: Write your story. I pray that you will live abundant lives walking with the Lord. Love people. Leave this world better because you were in it. We got your back. Fly!

To my Mama, from the side of the field in little league football to the chair beside my bed at Walter Reed, you've always been there. You've been my rock. Thank you.

To my Dad, my creativity, work ethic, toughness, grit, and so much more, I owe to you. You're also the best storyteller I know. You helped me become a man.

To all of the people who have helped me become the man I am today; thank you for investing your time, talents, and treasure into my life. It is with your example in my mind that I try to do the same for others.

To my fellow Iraq and Afghanistan combat veterans, I sincerely love you, even if I don't know you. Please don't waste your life. You still have so much to offer this country and this world. We may not be in the service anymore, but we can always serve.

Introduction

It is my experience that many of us in this current generation of Americans live in a foggy haze of "I don't know" and "I think so." For instance, if I were to ask any random person off the street if God is real, the majority answer would be one of the statements I just mentioned. These faithless answers would be the most common responses to another question as well: "Are you a good person?"

Well, are you a good person? Is God real? What if God is real, and He does not think that you are a good person? What does Jesus have to do with it? Are all religions the same? Does any of this really even matter? If you cannot definitively answer these questions then this book is for you.

I, too, know what it is like to feel as if we are in a boat that is adrift in a sea of subjective truth without an anchor to keep us where we are, without a rudder to guide our direction, and without a paddle to propel us forward. Eventually one may decide that the best choice is to jump overboard and start swimming as fast as you can, but then you realize that there is no land in sight. So you return to the floating prison cell, hoping that perhaps someone will come and save you. Your prayers are nothing more than messages in a bottle that you send out hoping that someone will read them. It does not have to be this way. There is a better way!

In this book, you will hear a true story—my story. I once had many questions and few answers. It took three tours of duty in Iraq, a near fatal explosion, and a whole lot of recovery to find the treasure I had been looking for. I'm thankful to be alive to tell my story, and I hope that God will richly bless each of you and change your lives to the point that you are riding in a chariot pulled by dolphins through the ocean where you were once adrift. And for all my boys out there who were in my platoons and fought beside me, GTB's for life! Hoodang baby! Black knights—you know!

"The kingdom of heaven is like treasure hidden in a field. When a man found it, he hid it again, and then in his joy went and sold all he had and bought that field." (Matthew 13:44 NIV)

Chapter 1
Between Two Trailers

If you should happen to find yourself in the possession of an actual Purple Heart award document, (that's the paper that they hand soldiers when they pin the medal on their chest) then you would see that the award was "established by General George Washington at Newburgh, New York, August 7, 1782." Strangely enough, a couple hundred years later I would be born in a small town in the foothills of the Carolina Mountains on Purple Heart Day. The best part is that I was about two weeks late. Bless my poor mama's heart for having to carry me around overtime in the dog days of summer. It is almost as if I were born to be a stubborn soldier.

My first memory that I can recollect here on earth is a good one, a peaceful and pure vision that has always stuck with me. I recall escaping my crib sometime early in the morning right around sunrise. I can remember that the trailer we lived in was not dark anymore, but there were no rays coming through the windows from the daytime sun. There was an old dresser—I say old because it looked like it came out of the sixties. It was an obnoxious tint of yellow or puke green, and I remember that the knobs on the drawers were some type of hippy looking flowers. I used those knobs to maneuver down the front of the dresser to reach the floor. There were also Smurfs, the little blue cartoon people, somewhere but that's probably irrelevant.

I was lonely, I suppose, as I made a beeline for the other side of the trailer where my parents were still sleeping. There was a wood-burning stove in the living room that was really scary for a little guy to look up at from the floor level. I had to make sure that I got by that fire-breathing monster quickly and then not look back until I had made it past the front door and into my parents' room. I made a break for it crawling all the way. I am not sure whether I

1

climbed into bed or if my dad scooped me up, but I know the next part for sure. I was nuzzled in between my parents. I felt safe.

The only other memory I have from this short period of my life, when my parents were together, was not as pleasant. I was in my bed, older this time, maybe around age three. The sounds of yelling and cursing came flowing through my doorway, which was illuminated by the light from the living room. Next, I see my mama with her back against the wall as she and my dad were going at it. Details are sketchy, but I can remember the door closing and the light of my room fading to dark as the screaming and bumping continued. I put my hands over my ears. I did not feel safe anymore.

After that my mom and I lived in a small trailer across the road from my dad, who remained in what used to be our family home. Our trailer had curtains instead of walls. It was like this. If I pulled a curtain closed, I had my own room; open the curtain, and I was in my mom's room; open all the curtains, and we're both in the living room. My early childhood was rather pleasant and carefree. I spent a lot of time in daycare, but that meant that even though I was an only child at the time, I had lots of kids to play with.

It is my theory that children are blessed to have the ability to adjust to any situation and be joyful. I can still remember the little Iraqi children we would see in the villages and along the roadsides, always smiling, always happy, even though bloodshed and chaos were waiting just a moment away. I look back fondly on these early years of my life, ages three to nine. I guess it was not the normal American family portrait, but it was all I knew. I lived with my mom and saw my dad every other weekend if it worked out. I was a happy kid. I played soccer, baseball, and football; I liked school, had tons of friends, and felt that life was good. Then things started to change. I see storm clouds on the horizon, but I don't have a shelter, poncho, or umbrella. I think things are about to get nasty.

Chapter 2
In A Nutshell

There are a lot of intricacies about life that one does not really understand as a child. We view the world from a completely different perspective before fully feasting upon the fruit from the tree of knowledge of good and evil. All I knew was that I was relatively happy and didn't really want anything to change. Sure, my mom worked all the time, and I was a little too comfortable being babysat by the television, but I remember not understanding why my dad was filing for custody of me. It just did not make any sense to me at all. From the worldview of a child these things can be misunderstood as the imagination of the young goes wild.

I suppose this was the first experience of war in my life, and what a ruthless battle it was. I did not know how to process it personally, so I blamed myself. With the memory of my parents sleeping peacefully together in my mind, along with the pictures of a happy young couple that I would see periodically as I aimlessly wandered through photo albums, I tried to figure out why these people who looked so blissful could now have so much hatred and bitterness towards each other. *It must have been my fault,* I thought. *They were fine before I came along and ruined everything.* This was the period in my life when things started to head south.

I loved my mama, and life with her was all I ever knew. Seeing her go through all of that and then finally lose the battle caused me to hold a great deal of resentment towards my dad. I desperately wanted to blame someone for the whole mess, and though I blamed myself for the divorce, the custody battle was all him. Nobody came out of that battle unscathed, and even after the war was over, there would be various pop shots and indirect fire incidents that would continue. Comparisons could be drawn to reflect our family issues in the plight of everyone involved in

Operation Iraqi Freedom. Even after the initial invasion was concluded, the fighting had only begun.

As of this real-world moment, writing this story, I am currently blessed to have two living parents, and the last thing I would want to do is dishonor them by splashing a lot of ugly details around that are not necessary to get the point across. It was a hurtful time. Now that I am a father myself, the details and motivations of the situation are more comprehensible. But either way, I found my life flipped upside down as I began to live with my dad shortly before middle school. Looking back, I kind of feel bad for him; I had clearly planted my flag in loyalty to my mom and painted him as the bad guy in the whole situation. In his defense, it must have been hard to raise a son who hates your guts.

While living at my dad's, everything began to feel much more awkward. Life became a struggle, and I suppose it showed, as I started to put on extra pounds and began dealing with the fun of being one of the only fat kids among young adolescent southern males. I quickly became an easy target for bullying as a chubby kid with self-esteem issues. Imagine a 200lb 6th grader with glasses, a bowl cut hair-do, baggy blue jeans, a Nike Penn State sweatshirt, and some way too expensive Damon Stoudamire basketball sneakers. I don't even remember who the player was, nor did I play basketball, but I thought those sneakers were tight! Like I said, I was an easy target. Even though I lived with my dad, my mama always got me the gear I wanted, even those big legged JNCO jeans when I was having a trying-to-dress-like-a-skater-even-though-I didn't-skate phase.

The junior high years were probably some of the hardest years of my life. For lack of a better word, they sucked. To illustrate, I will tell a story within a story: I woke up late, just a few minutes before the school bus was scheduled to arrive. I threw on my clothes, did a five-second toothbrush just to kill the morning breath, grabbed my unnecessarily heavy backpack, and made a break for the front door. As I came outside, I could hear the rumble of the engine as the

4

school bus made its approach up the steep hill. It was only one stop away from our house! From the front porch, there was about fifty yards to the end of the driveway, and the driver lady was not going to sit there and wait all day. In fact, the driver would stop for one second, put her flashers on, and if she did not see you then she was out of there. You were lucky if you got that.

So I made a break for it across the yard. I could see the flashing yellow lights through the trees as it got closer and closer to the mailbox. I do not remember whether it was rainy, foggy, a frost, or if we had a little snow on the ground, but for some weather-related reason, the grass was a little slick that day. Just as the driver was stopping, I burst through the pine trees at the end of the yard! Right before you get to the street there is a small hill that drops down into a shallow irrigation ditch next to the road. Directly next to the side of the bus I lose my feet sliding down the hill on my right thigh and butt cheek. I try to jump up quickly, gather myself, and knock some of the mud off my pants as I can already hear all of the kids on the bus laughing at my clumsy, clearly unintentional, baseball slide down the hill.

Embarrassed and obviously rattled, I began the long walk down the center aisle of the bus to the back where I usually sat with the other kids my age I knew from the neighborhood. Folks got their giggles and their jeers in as I passed by the rows where they were sitting. I took my seat and the chatter calmed down to the normal tone for a bus full of kids. Perhaps a few minutes passed and my "friend" said that he smelled something. Better yet, he said it so obnoxiously loud that even the driver at the front of the bus could hear it; "Eeeeewwwww! I smell ****," and everyone started to check their shoes to see if perhaps someone had stepped in it. Pedro identified that the smell was coming from me, and I soon realized that it was not mud that I had all over my pants, shirt, and backpack. Nope, apparently, I had slid through a giant pile of dog POOP!

Pedro led the pack as everyone in the vicinity started to run forward in the bus to get away from me. It was like I had leprosy or was patient zero in a zombie apocalypse movie. When we arrived at school, after probably the longest bus ride of my life, the bus driver escorted me into the office where I had to try to contact someone to bring me new clothes. Of course, in the era before cell phones, I could not get a hold of either of my parents, and the only option was that one of my family members would be able to bring me some in a couple hours. The administrators decided to take me out back and hose the poop off of my clothes while I waited. This was junior high in a nutshell.

My personal conduct began to continuously decline throughout seventh and eighth grade as I plummeted from "A" honor roll to "No" honor roll. I had already started smoking, drinking, and viewing pornography. I had begun to idolize the thugs and gangsters that I would see in the rap videos on MTV. It turns out that letting your twelve-year-old boy run the streets day and night all summer long, unsupervised, is not conducive to good adolescent character development.

In school, I did not really feel like I fit in anywhere. Even though I was fairly smart and capable of making good grades all throughout elementary school, I did not feel like I fit in with the smart kids. I played football, but I did not really click with other guys on the team. I started to realize that I would be an outcast, and so I tossed my chips in with the rejects, troublemakers, and lost boys.

I got sentenced to three days of in-school suspension for selling cigarettes in the bathroom between classes. One time, I pushed a kid down in guitar class, and of course, he fell on the bridge of one of the guitars and broke it in half. It was actually not malicious; I was just messing around. Either way, I ended up getting in pretty big trouble for that. It was determined that because I was too young to have an official job, and I begged in tears to not charge my dad for the replacement. I would work off the price of the guitar as restitution. Every day after school, I worked for two hours at five bucks per hour. So I guess it took me about a month to pay it off.

Thanks for that, by the way, Mrs. Principal lady. It was a good life lesson!

Chapter 3
In His Image

You may be asking the question, "Where is God in all of this?" I look back at this time in life as a miserable slice of my existence, but it was not all bad, and looking back from where I am today, I can see God moving even in the midst of my personal tribulation. There were people who had a powerful presence for good in my life as the battle for my soul raged all around me. I am becoming increasingly aware that God likes to use people to do His work in the world. The Holy Spirit spoke through men to bring forth the Word of God. Jesus changed the world through the lives of twelve disciples. Don't get me started on Abraham, Moses, King David, Paul, and the super servant Himself, Jesus Christ. God's Spirit works through people who love Him; of this I am sure. I guess this would be the tribute section of the story.

For example, I firmly believe that He put an angel in our home to keep me going and to keep my dad and me from killing each other. Looking back, I really do not know if I would have made it through adolescence without her presence in the situation. Well, maybe she was not an angel, but a godsend, nonetheless. Barbara married my dad when I was around twelve years old, and she would sacrificially serve as cook, maid, and mediator in a home full of bitterness and chaos until I was out of the house and well established in my Army career.

I think I learned more about spirituality from Barbara than from any other person on earth. She was really something! I think my stepmom had probably lived the lives of ten men by the time our paths crossed. Barbara had spent time as a nun, married a millionaire, taught English literature to kids in inner-city Chicago, was a national champion in dressage (that's the fancy horse riding where they kind of trot and dance), several times a cancer survivor, and so much more. At approximately five feet tall and ninety-three pounds soaking wet, Barbara was a bite-sized superhero.

I knew lots of church people, but there was something different about Barbara's relationship with God. It was real to her. She didn't go to church so that people would think that she was a good person. She legitimately loved God and wanted to spend time alone with her Creator. Just like Moses served as mediator between God and a nation of Israelites, who were constantly rebellious, Barbara was the only shot of peace and consistency in our household. I do not have the words to describe, and I'm perhaps only starting to realize, just how much of an impact she had, and continues to have, on my life.

Barbara died a couple of years ago. Cancer finally got the best of her after she had defeated it at least twice before. We had lost contact over the years, but I received word through a mutual acquaintance that she was not doing well. It was a real blessing that I was able to spend some time with her before she passed. We hugged, and I gave her a completely inadequate one-page letter in an attempt to let her know how thankful I was for her being such a powerful force for good in my life. I felt completely at peace as I left her apartment next to the nursing home where she was receiving Hospice care. I have no doubt that she is with the Lord. She was looking forward to the meeting, and even though she was weary, there was joy in her heart.

Another presence of the Lord throughout my life has been my grandmother. GG, as she is now known, is one of my favorite people on planet earth. As I look back upon my story, she is sprinkled into the background of so many good memories in the midst of terrible times. I am her oldest grandchild, and I think that I am her favorite grandson, which is completely OK with me. A picture of selflessness the entire time I have known her, GG has always been there for me.

It is such a blessing to have people like her in our lives and communities. These types of people represent the salt and light of the world, and without them, this world is a dark, rotten, and mean place. Papa and GG always cared for me like their own son. They could not have been more supportive, and it must have been a burden to them, financially and emotionally. I lived at their house for weeks at a time and never can I remember being treated negatively in any way. They came to my games, took me to church, listened to me sing, and took me everywhere I needed to go. My favorite memory of GG is when she would ask what I wanted for my birthday, and I always wanted the same thing. Every year for probably five years in a row, GG and I would head to the mall and she would get me some new husky size blue jeans and maybe a couple of shirts before school started a few days later. We would go grab lunch and just hang out together. She's my buddy.

As you might imagine, I was a pretty high-maintenance kid, but GG's love never wavered. In the midst of trauma she was always a presence of love, grace, encouragement, devotion, and faith. When my dad got stabbed shortly after I moved in with him, I was pretty messed up about it—understandably so—and I was experiencing thoughts and emotions that were really difficult to process and deal with for a ten-year-old boy. Evil had made a distinct appearance into my world, and it had shaken up an already fragile kid. I cannot really remember much from that time, and I am not sure why, but I can clearly recall good people who were in my corner when the sky was falling down on top of me, and there is no greater blessing. The world needs more people like GG—of this I am also certain.

The world could also use more Shizzles. When I was going through my awkward early adolescent years, I came across another chubby misfit like myself. I was in one of the summer youth plays that they host in our area every year. Folks that knew me in my later years, especially the Iraq days, would never have guessed it, but I was in a few plays as a kid. Go ahead—laugh it up fellas. In one of these summer youth productions, I met Shizzle. As with many great friendships, we started off as enemies. I was a weird and often annoying kid, and I could see how I would not be the first pick of dudes to pal around with. I certainly would not gain you any popularity points at this point in life. There is also the thumb tack incident.

I guess it was "Joseph and the Amazing Technicolor Dream Coat" that we were presenting. I had probably thoroughly gotten on everyone's nerves, especially the teenagers, but my reputation for excessive awkwardness was not yet set in stone. While we were doing the dress rehearsal, I was messing around off to the side of the stage, and for some reason I was holding a thumbtack in my teeth. I don't know if anybody can remember this, but there was a pro wrestler named Razor Ramon back in the day. He used to walk around with a toothpick hanging out of his mouth, and I thought he was "too cool, man!" So maybe that is what I was shooting for. I don't remember whether someone startled me or if I was just playing with the thumbtack in my mouth, but I swallowed it…

"Freaked out" does not adequately describe the emotions I felt at the time. Visions of being ambulanced to the ER for an emergency removal operation, where they would rip me open from my belly button to my throat, started to bounce around in my head. In my worried panic, I am not sure who I told first—it may have been Shizzle—but within the first few minutes, every actor in the play knew about it. Needless to say, I was now known as "the fat kid who swallowed a thumbtack." The tack was never seen again. Gross. It's been about twenty years now, so I am assuming that it worked itself out—hopefully.

A few years afterward, I was loitering outside of the coffee shop downtown, where some of the artsy kids would hang on Friday nights, including some cute females. I ran into Shizzle, and he immediately recognized me as the "kid who swallowed that thumbtack." If somebody from the future would have teleported through time and space to tell me that Shizzle would end up being my most devoted and loyal friend, fifteen-year-old me would have laughed in their face. They would have been right, but I will explain this later as the story unfolds.

My point is that God likes to use people made in His image to make an impact in the lives of other people. If we have the good fortune of being able to think of anybody in our life who has never stabbed us in the back, spoke evil of us, or aired our dirty laundry for all to see, then we are surely blessed. Our utmost goal should be to serve as this type of blessing in the lives of as many people as possible. As the story moves forward, keep an eye out for the people that make seemingly coincidental guest appearances over and over again to save the day in large and small ways.

Chapter 4
Bullies

As I mentioned before, being a victim of bullying was a pretty consistent and regular occurrence throughout my adolescence. One incident was particularly damaging and would serve as a turning point in my life. It was not a positive change but a turning point, nonetheless. It was freshman year in high school, and I was looking forward to leaving the troublesome years of junior high behind in search of a fresh start. It didn't pan out exactly as I had hoped.

The bell rang for lunch, and all of us piled out of freshman English, herded like cattle into the hallways and down to the cafeteria. In my peripheral, I see this little kid get slammed into the lockers a few yards down the hall from our door. He was a new guy who had just come to our school from somewhere in Georgia—the state, not the country. The new kid, also a freshman, was maybe a hundred pounds of bones on his best day. The tough guy, who was a senior if I recall correctly, was approximately 200 pounds of lean muscle and knew how to handle himself.

I did not even think about it. I just intervened in an attempt to save the ragdoll that was being abused against the lockers. The tough guy's attention was immediately redirected towards me as he said, "You want some too?" I, of course, declined his gracious offer. I explained that my only intention was to break it up because it was unfair. By this point, the teachers had become aware of the altercation, quickly dispersed the crowd, and encouraged us to move toward the lunchroom. The show was over... or so I thought.

By the time I entered through the double red doors of the high school cafeteria, most of the other kids were already sitting with their trays. It was mostly freshmen who were lined up into two columns, waiting to receive our share of delectable treats. By the way, I'm not picky when it comes to chow. It is referred to as the seafood diet. I see food; I eat it. Did I mention that in my freshman year I was at my fattest? Yup. At approximately 5'9 and 245lbs of whatever the opposite of muscle is, I thought my self-esteem could not get any lower. I was wrong.

I decided to go over to the main food line to the left, where a few kids that I was cool with were standing. They quickly started to ask me about the altercation in the hallway minutes earlier. As I started to describe the prior events, the tough guy, unbeknownst to me, walked up behind me just in time to hear his name come out of my mouth. The start of the festivities is a little blurry, but I think he pretty loudly stated, "Oh now you talking **** about me?" I turned around to face him, and he pushed me in the chest with enough force to knock me into the kids standing behind me. I am thankful they were there, because otherwise I would have fallen on my butt before getting beaten to a pulp. I gathered myself, and for the sake of pride, not trying to look like a wimp in front of literally the entire school, I went to push him back.

It turned out to be a bad decision as he quickly snatched me down by the back of the shirt and started to beat the left side of my head with his fist. I am not sure why I didn't fight back. Maybe I was more scared of having to tell my dad that I was suspended for five days from school (which is the automatic zero-tolerance penalty for fighting)? Or maybe I was afraid that if I fought back, the beating would be much more substantial? Getting hit in the side of the head is a lot better than getting punched in the face, that's for sure. Whether actively or inactively, I decided to cover my face, take it, and wait it out until someone decided to intervene on my behalf. It took a while, but eventually the gym coach came over and pulled the tough guy off of me. I never lost consciousness, but I took a pretty vicious beating.

Because I never actually laid a hand on the tough guy, there was no punitive action against me for the incident. Unfortunately, the tough guy was expelled because of it and was forced to attend an alternative school. This popular and athletic force of nature was

14

no longer able to attend our school, and it was all my fault in the eyes of his comrades. I walked the halls in fear for the rest of that year worrying that some other senior would seek to do me harm as an act of retribution.

There were times in this period of my life when I contemplated suicide. I felt that I had no worth, that life would never get any better, and that everyone would be better off without me. Late one night, I thought about the loaded .45 auto that was hidden above my dad's bed. I walked into his bedroom and was going to do it right there in the doorway. *Why wait?* It was locked, cocked, and ready to rock, as a soldier might say. I placed it to my temple and closed my eyes tightly. The tears fell down my cheeks. I remember my breathing being heavy, like the panicky anticipation of receiving an immunization at the doctor's office when you were a kid.

I don't know if I would call it a voice, but it was not something that I had experienced before in life. I guess I had experienced spiritual emotions at times, but never "the Still Small Voice." It was as if I was hearing someone speak to me saying, "Don't do it. It will get better. Just keep going." I was not looking for attention, reaching out for help, or just messing around. Nope. I had reached my limit of emotional pain, and I was going to actually blow my brains out. But this experience, which I firmly believe to be divine intervention, gave me the encouragement that I needed to move forward.

I began to see things in a new light. The following summer I would turn fifteen, and in South Carolina, that meant one thing: I could drive. But a man cannot drive his tennis shoes, so I was going to need a ride. In order to acquire said vehicle, a man must have money. As we are well aware, the best way to get money is to get a job. So that's what I did. Picking peaches and washing dishes was my claim to fame. By the end of the summer, I had saved enough to buy my very own 1985 Honda accord.

The cool thing about transitions in life is that they give you an opportunity to remake yourself to a certain extent. This is what work and the freedom that comes with a driver's license gave me. The seniors holding animosity toward me with my beat down in their memories would no longer be at school. I was around new people at work in area restaurants, and I could now have friends who weren't from my neighborhood or school. I decided to become a tough guy.

I wanted to get as far away from that innocent, sweet-hearted, self-loathing, fat kid as I could. I was tired of getting picked on, tired of being at the bottom of the totem pole, tired of not getting girls, and tired of being too ashamed to even look at myself in the mirror. I hit the gym, started to train hard for football and wrestling, and tried to pick up some boxing training along the way. I wanted my reputation to be different. I wanted some respect. In the first semester of junior year, I found out how I was going to get it.

It was the morning of September 11, 2001. We were in English class when a commotion started to brew. "We are under attack!" These were the words of the teacher who knocked on the door before barging in to tell us what was happening. I didn't understand at first, but when the teacher turned on the television it became clear. I saw the second plane hit the tower. I saw the people falling to their deaths on the cement below as they attempted to get away from the intense heat and heavy smoke of the explosions that had blocked their way out of the buildings. I watched the towers collapse, burying New York's finest public servants in rubble and debris.

Tears began to flow as I looked at the fear of the unknown and worry about future attacks in the eyes of my classmates. According to what I read in various sources, around three thousand civilians died that day. Innocent people just doing their jobs and going about their everyday lives were suddenly snuffed out by a sucker punch from the Middle East. I can understand the Pentagon hit, because everyone in that building knew that they were working on a potential military target. Those people had signed the dotted line, knowing that they might put life and limb in jeopardy for their

16

nation. But the towers, nah, that's a different story. Somebody was going to have to answer for that. I decided that the first time I got beat up by a bully, without fighting back, was going to be my last. This bully was going to have to pay for this, and I was going to do my part to make sure that he did. I suppose in that moment, I knew where I was headed and what I was going to do. I was going to be a soldier.

Chapter 5
The Waiting Game

Even though I had decided that I was going to be a soldier, I held some slight optimism, delusional as it may have been, that I may be offered an athletic scholarship for football. In reality, I had no shot, but you know how irrational sixteen-to-seventeen-year-old boys can be. I loved football and had played the sport since third grade. But I was slow, had the agility of an injured sloth, stiff hips, chicken legs, knock-knees, and a two-point-something GPA. I do not know who I was kidding, probably only me. Even though I lacked all of the natural athletic attributes, I was a pretty good player and started on the varsity offensive line from sophomore year onward. It was a small 1A high school with only a few hundred kids in it, so there was not the greatest pool of talent to draw from. At a larger school, I probably would have ridden the pine.

I was a hard worker, and I always tried my best. I was the epitome of an "effort guy." I cried after every game, whether we won or lost. I always left it all on the field, and after the game, I would find myself flooded with overwhelming emotions. With a tremendous chip on my shoulder, I desperately wanted to prove myself, and being on the football team was one of the only times in my life that I felt valued, like I mattered, like I made a difference. A youth pastor I talked to recently told me, "Teenagers basically only want two things: to feel loved and to feel special." I think he was probably spot on.

You probably noticed that there was an absence of adult male role models in the tribute chapter. They had fairly limited and temporary roles in my life, but these men made a strong and lasting impact on the man I would later become. I am assuredly biased and have been exposed to a loaded sample because of being raised in the south, but I truly believe that Godly, Christian, American men are the best guys on earth. In my years, I have met many extraordinarily good men, and most of them love Jesus and love America. But as I said, this could never pass for an objective analysis.

An example of this is the character displayed by my high school football coach. Do not think for a second that our coach was some kind of softy, a doormat, or a pushover, because he was pretty far from any of those things. He would grab you by the facemask and tear you up one side and down the other. But it was only when you needed it or had earned it, and if he felt like he was too hard on you or out of line, he would apologize. Real men know how to say they're sorry. I learned so much about what it means to be a leader, and a man, from Coach.

One night I was driving home, not sure where I was coming from, but it was raining pretty bad. It was late, because I remember that it was already completely dark. I saw someone walking with a brisk and angry stride up the side of the road, and I am glad I was not going faster because I probably would have hit him. I pulled beside and lowered my window to see if I could give the guy a ride. It was one of the other players from our team. Will was a grade behind me in school, and I do not know the entirety of the situation, but he was having some problems at home and decided to leave. He was clearly upset, and I did not know what to do, needing to get home myself. I called Coach.

They talked for a minute on the phone, and then Will handed the phone back to me with Coach still on the other end of the line. His words were, "Bring him to my house. I'll give you some gas money when you get here." It was probably 11:00 pm on a school night. Coach had two young kids and a wife of his own to worry about. I could think of about ten different excuses off the top of my head, reasons to make Will someone else's problem, but Coach went above and beyond what was expected of him. His job was to coach football, but Coach's purpose was to be a good man and to lead others to become the same.

The football dream for me came to an abrupt and complete end with one minute and fifty-two seconds left on the clock in the fourth quarter of the last game my senior year. It was the playoffs, and if I am not mistaken, we were losing 45-7. I guess Coach was letting us seniors play it out and go down in a blaze of glory. I am sure he knew that for most of us this would be the last game of organized football we would ever play.

I cannot remember the play we called, but I remember my end of it pretty well to this day. I fired off the ball and engaged the defensive lineman. It was a stalemate, and I could see the outside linebacker coming in my peripheral. The tight-end picked up the block nicely and took the guy off of his feet. Unfortunately he landed on the back of my knee causing it to buckle beneath me. When I went down, the lineman I was engaged with bowled me over backwards while my leg was still pinned beneath the linebacker. There was a loud pop in the inside of my knee, and whatever hopes I had of playing football at the next level were gone.

In my mind, I knew that I just had to coast out the rest of my senior year, rehab my knee, graduate, not go to jail, and the Army would be waiting for me. I started partying hard. My buddy and I would meet up early to drink and do drugs before school. As soon as school was over, I was right back at it. Without football, getting messed up and acting crazy were the only things that made me feel good. Having the drugs and alcohol made me popular for the first time in my life. All of a sudden everybody wanted me around, when just a year or two earlier they didn't even talk to me.

It started to get pretty heavy towards the end of my senior year. I had developed an intimate relationship with cocaine, and it really had me hooked pretty hard. I just could not get enough of the stuff, and eventually, it was taking all my money from my dishwashing job to supply my habit, so I went down the dark and dangerous road of making money in less legal ways. Suddenly, I had become the guy I wanted to be; I was popular; I had money; I could fight; guys were intimidated by me; and females were becoming increasingly interested in me. Oh yeah, I was a tough guy now.

It was a miracle that I was able to finish high school and actually be able to join the Army virtually unscathed, as far as paperwork is concerned. Well, it probably does not count as an official miracle, but I have no doubt that God preserved me through those times of negligence and stupidity for a time later in life.

Because I got messed up before school and subsequently went to sleep in first period every day throughout second semester, it turned out that I was failing a math class I needed to graduate. Isn't it funny how that works out? (By the way, Mrs. Teacher Lady, that was very disrespectful and I apologize.) I needed to make a C on the final exam to pass the class. So, of course, I spent the whole night cramming for it…. Nope, I ended up partying the night before until about four in the morning, oversleeping, and showing up thirty minutes late for the final.

This is when I witnessed and experienced one of the best examples of grace. As it turns out, I did not make the grade I needed to make on that exam. I was just a few points short. I had passed the exam, but when averaged with my poor marks from the rest of the semester, I was one point short; I had failed. This was going to ruin everything! I had already signed a contract with the Army. I was supposed to ship off to basic in less than two months, and if I had to complete summer school, it would put me in breach of my contract.

I went to the assistant principle, who accompanied me to talk with the teacher. I deserved to fail. Even if it was by one point, I had earned it. I knew what was at stake, and I partied all night. I showed up drunk for crying out loud! All I could do was beg for mercy because I knew I had no case. It turns out that there was a grading curve added to the exam, which gave me the points necessary, and I was allowed to graduate with my class. I am extremely grateful. Grace: unmerited favor I did not deserve.

Another example of God's preservation is the time we had a big ole going away party for yours truly. It was the 4th of July, and I was about ten days out from shipping off to basic. Everyone met up in the parking lot of a local grocery store, and we convoyed to the hunting cabin out in the country. My best friends were there, lots of booze, fireworks, the whole nine yards. Once the festivities had really got swinging, a cop car showed up. Apparently, some of my friends had been shooting fireworks at the cows across the road or something like that.

Either way, my best friend from high school and I went on down to talk to the cops. It was not to seem valiant or anything, but mainly so the rest of the underage drinkers would have some time to hide the alcohol and, in some cases, themselves, in the woods. Plus, it was my dad and my buddy's step-dad who were on the deed to the hunting cabin. Ultimately, the responsibility was going to fall on us regardless. They asked how old we were, and I could feel the blood rushing from my face, as I knew they were on to us. I replied that I was seventeen, and that we were having a little going away party because I was shipping off to basic soon. I hoped that playing the Army card would woo them in my favor. Then out came the Breathalyzer.

I was petrified with the thought that after I played my song on that trumpet the whole world was going to come crashing down around me. As I blew into the Breathalyzer, I had visions of sitting in the back of the police car as the county boys raided the house. I imagined all of the interesting things that would have been left behind by the teenagers who scattered like roaches into the woods. There's no telling what they might find in there, I thought. Worst of all, I figured that all of this unclaimed property would undoubtedly be charged to yours truly. Well, let's get this over with. I blew a .17. Yes kids, that's a little over double the driving limit and exactly .17 more than you are allowed to have in your blood if your blood happens to be less than twenty-one years of age. I was surprised, because in that moment, I was feeling quite sober and alert. I just knew I was in for it.

The two officers were figuring out what they were going to do next. Then something unexpected happened. Just about the time I was going to be cuffed, a call came across the radio that there had been shots fired downtown where the 4th of July celebration was wrapping up. This apparently took precedence over a party with a bunch of recently graduated teens. They asked us if we had any designated drivers. We quickly located the only two people we knew who did not drink. Of course, like the angel on my shoulder, Shizzle was one of the two who saved the day by blowing double zeros on the breathalyzer. Then one of the cops looked dead at me and said, "Cut the crap. If we have to come back out here, you're going to jail." Then he looked to his partner, and after a consenting head nod, they rolled out to fry bigger fish. We did not see them again.

To be perfectly honest, I barely tripped out the front door of the local high school. I barely stumbled into the Army by the skin of my teeth. I ended up running with people who had a negative impact on my life, but it was ultimately because I sought them out. For others, I was the bad person that negatively impacted their life. If you happened to be one of my close friends in the year leading up to basic training, then your life is probably worse because of my influence. For this, I also apologize. I was lost.

Chapter 6
Meet my side chick, Jesus

It seemed to me that church was just basically a big get together, like a social club, where everybody got dressed up to come show off, brag about their kids and accomplishments, sing, listen to a guy talk, and then when no one could take the boredom anymore, they wrapped it up with one last song, and out the doors they went. I personally had always believed that there was a God or gods, and I was fully aware that I was not Him, Her, or one of Them. It just seemed silly to me that a universe could create itself from nothing, and it still does. Obviously there had to be something more out there, but I could not figure out exactly what or whom.

I can remember sitting in a small Baptist church with my mama listening to a fire and brimstone sermon coming loudly from the red-faced preacher in the front of the congregation. Being still a small child, I had no idea about the dangers and ramifications of sin, the deity of Christ, or even the significance of the cross and resurrection. But, being presented with a choice between spending eternity in heaven or hell, I felt like the decision was easy. Let's see, forever in the joyful bliss of paradise or being tormented in darkness and flames for the rest of eternity. Yeah, I'll take option A. So, at the age of six to eight, not sure, I made my first profession of faith and was submersed in baptism. I do not know if I could say that I was saved at that point in time, and certainly do not want to get into a long theological discourse about it. But from that point forward, Jesus was always somewhere in my life, just not usually anywhere prominent or important.

I think that a lot of people who claim to believe in Jesus live like this. We do pretty much whatever we want, and then fit Jesus into an hour at the end of the weekend to make ourselves feel better, or maybe, to make people think we are better than we really are. This is the type of Christian I was. I went down the aisles at a Billy

Graham crusade. I said the prayer. I guess it was mainly about what people would think if I did not go down. Other people I knew were going, and I did not want them to think I didn't believe. After all, I knew I was a sinner.

Did I believe that Jesus was the Son of God? Yes. Did I believe that He died on a cross for the sins of the world? Yes. Did I believe that God raised Him from the dead? Yes. Some would say that by believing these are historical facts, and not myths, this would ensure that I was saved. But was Jesus the Lord of my life? No. Was I obedient to Him in any way, shape, or form? Was I a disciple? No way. Not even close.

I was involved in my church as a youth all the way up to my senior year of high school, and I even sang in the contemporary Christian group at the early service. But was it about God? Was it worship? Probably not, maybe a little, but mostly it was about my own selfish desires. I liked to sing, and I liked when people liked my singing. There were pretty girls who sang with the group, and I liked pretty girls. There was also a sense that I was needed, and everybody likes to feel valued. I also liked that most of the people in the church thought of me as a good boy who sang in the band, played football, went to Sunday school, and was going to go defend our nation after high school. The truth is that I was partying and having sex out of wedlock with my girlfriend all night on Saturday, then using drugs to wake up in the morning to go sing praises to the Lord. I was a carnal, weak, shallow, and lukewarm believer at best, who knew nothing of being a disciple of Jesus Christ and could not have cared less.

My main chick was pleasure, selfish desire, and ego. I had a girlfriend who broke my heart. She taught me a lesson about my relationship with God that I would not really understand until years down the road. I was going to marry her. We were going to have kids together, and she was going to be there with me wherever the Army sent me. She was the one; I just knew it. Sure, we had only been dating for a month or so, but who cares? I was hooked bad. I loved to go places with her, and tell everybody that she was mine, show her off like a trophy that proved I was not the weird fat kid I used to be.

She was going to wait for me and keep herself pure and faithful while I was away. When I returned with a bank account full of money, we would get married and travel the globe together as I saved the world with a machine gun. Oh what bliss! It's amazing how our minds can be filled with such make-believe ideas.

I guess, I was about a month into basic training when I found out she had cheated on me. It messed me up pretty bad, and my heart grew colder that day. I was able to make a phone call the following Sunday, after receiving the letters from multiple friends who notified me of her infidelities. She admitted to it, and our relationship was over. I was so mad. I had given her my heart, and she just stepped on it. Ultimately, I realized that I was a fool blinded by lust and selfish pride.

The same day, or not long after, I received the letters from multiple people notifying me of her betrayal, a strange thing happened. I had just read the letters for the third or fourth time, and I was about to lose it. I needed to drop my run time for the PT test, and being a fat kid my whole life mixed with the knee injury from months earlier, it was not going well. In order to let off some steam and also get some fitness, I "killed two birds with one stone" by going downstairs to the drill pad to go for a run.

Strangely enough, as I was running, a kid from first platoon came out of the stairwell and looked straight at me. I started to go around him, when, out of nowhere, he ran towards me and tried to kick me in the chest like King Leonidas in the movie *300*. My momentum pushed him backwards, as his kick was highly ineffective and poorly planned. I still do not know why he did it. I do not remember ever seeing the kid before in my life. I threw one punch connecting with the left side of his head right above the ear. He fell into the bleachers and hit the other side of his head. As he was lying there on the cement bleeding from both sides of his head, I felt a power I had not known before. It felt good.

Don't get me wrong, by this point in my life I had been in a few fights, and it was not the first time I had won. But it was the first time I had knocked someone out, and it was the first time I could remember channeling anger from within me into violence against another person. I was not mad at that kid. I was mad at the girl who broke my heart, my dad, the tough guy who beat me up freshman year, and maybe even mad at God for the way my life had turned out.

Basic training really taught me a lot about my real relationship with God. Back home I was in church every Sunday. Now that I was away from everybody who knew me, there was no need to go to church. You did not impress other soldiers by going to church and acting like a "good boy." Nope. You impress other soldiers by proving that you are a force to be reckoned with.

In the Army, you can tell who the real Christians are, because they have nothing to gain from other people by going to church, reading their Bible, or living a Christ centered life. In fact, it can be detrimental to be a genuine Christian in the Army, because in our spare time many soldiers are pursuing ungodly things like wild parties, excessive drinking, brawling, one-night stands, and all the fun consequences that come along with living in debauchery. If a guy does not participate in these types of things, then he becomes the oddball that is always alone in their barracks room on Friday night reading a book.

I wanted to be liked, feared, and respected by those around me. I had the attitude of "you don't like me, then you better fear and respect me." I had a heart that had grown callous and cold. I was done trusting people and trying to do the right thing. I had decided that I was going to look out for number one from this point forward. I pushed Jesus to the side so much that He was really not even in the picture anymore, or so I thought.

27

Looking back now, and we all know how hindsight works, I can see that I had done to Jesus what my girlfriend had done to me. I had confessed Him as Lord, but I was cheating on Him in every facet of my life. He had looked out for me and helped me out time after time. Otherwise, I would have flunked out of high school, gone to jail, voided my contract, and knocked up my cheating girlfriend. Ouch!

After basic training, I was stationed in Germany. By the way, parents do not let your eighteen-year-old run around unsupervised in Germany. I knew I was going to Iraq in a few months, so I figured I better have as much fun as I could while I had the chance. I had fun; there is no doubt about that. But the hardest day of my life was coming and fun was not going to help me then. What little faith I had was going to be tested, and this time there was not going to be a curve on the exam.

Chapter 7
Lost Boy

There is an Old Cherokee Indian proverb about two wolves. It matches up pretty well with the battle between the flesh and the spirit that the Apostle Paul wrote about often in his various letters to the churches. Here's how it goes:

An older Cherokee is teaching his grandson lessons about life. He says to the boy, "There is a battle raging inside of me." The youngster, with his interest sparked, asks, "What kind of battle, Grandfather?" The grandfather goes on to explain to the boy that it is a terrible and constant fight between two wolves. One wolf is evil, representing anger, bitterness, arrogance, ego, resentment, selfish desires, and the like. The other wolf is good, representing those things that are pure and beautiful in the world like truth, compassion, empathy, kindness, patience, gentleness, generosity, love, and joy. The boy then asks his grandfather, "Which one wins?" The grandfather replies, "The one you feed."

I will now tell you a story that illustrates the state of affairs in my heart as I prepared for my first deployment in Iraq. You tell me, which wolf was winning?

It was New Year's Eve, and I had just finished celebrating my first Christmas outside the United States. Although a couple days late, I had received my Christmas presents from my mama. You'll remember that I told you earlier that my mama always kept me squared away with the clothes I wanted. As I prepared to go out for the evening festivities, I laid out my brand-new outfit that I had bought with my enlistment bonus money. Yes. In 2003, they would give you a bonus of up to $20,000 for joining the right MOS—that's Army lingo for whatever your job is. Beside the outfit, I laid a silver shoe box; I did not even want to take the shoes out of the box until it was time to leave the barracks lest they be scuffed or lose their new-shoe smell. They were about the hottest pair of AND1 basketball sneakers I had ever seen. They were black suede with glossy black trim. I love my mama, and it was the first Christmas I had been away from her in my life. Those shoes meant a lot to me.

Most of the folks in our unit had gone home for Christmas block leave, but because us "newbooties" had taken leave after basic, we did not have any vacation days left to use. So, it was myself, my two buddies, and my German girlfriend who went out that night, and the drinking quickly got heavy. We had already finished a bucket of Long Island iced tea and were well into the second when, just like in basic, a total stranger decided to mess with me. The four of us were in a booth next to the pool table drinking and joking, when this guy I had never seen before walked up to us. He looked me straight in my eye and then stepped on my brand new AND1 sneakers. He not only stepped on them, but also twisted the ball of his foot on top of my shoe like someone putting out a cigarette butt they had just thrown on the ground. I flipped out, man!

I jumped up in his face and then pushed him down onto the pool table. *You gonna disrespect me? In front of my girl? In front of my boys?* Just when I was really about to jump on that pool table and give him the business, I felt a powerful force snatch me backwards. It was Big Kobe, the bar's highly capable bouncer. Imagine Michael Clark Duncan from the movie *The Green Mile*, except darker with an African accent and wearing a Kobe Bryant Lakers Jersey. I'm no little guy, but Big Kobe snatched me up and carried me off under his massive arm like I was a misbehaving toddler. He sat me down over next to the dance floor and put his huge finger in my face, as he let me know there would be no fighting in the club that night.

I went back to my booth after conceding that I would not be a problem for him anymore that evening, but my blood was boiling, my shoes were irreparably scuffed, and on top of all that, the guy who did it kept staring at me from across the room. With my entourage questioning my manhood as this punk continuously smirked while tossing winks in our direction, I could resist the temptation no longer.

There were two different ways to get to the bathroom from the booth where we were seated. You could take an immediate right and maneuver along the outside of the dance floor, past the bar and then hang a left at the stairs that led to the front door. Or you could take the shortcut to the left around the pool table, directly past the taunting punk, and the bathroom would be immediately in front of you. Route A would be the path of the peacemaker who does not want any problems. It was a few extra steps, but nobody would get hurt. Route B, on the other hand, was shorter, but it led to certain confrontation and conflict. I took Route B. I didn't even say a word to my girlfriend or my buddies at the table; I just got up and headed for the bathroom.

As I walked up to the punk, we never broke eye contact. I calmly said to him, "I'm gonna go take a piss. You can meet me outside." I half-heartedly expected to get hit from behind while I was indisposed at the urinal. As I left the bathroom, I looked toward the barstool where the guy had been sitting. Noticing that it was now empty, I turned to the left and went straight for the long flight of stairs that led up to the front door and the cobblestone streets. My adrenaline was pumping and mixing well with the copious amount of alcohol that I had ingested. I wondered what awaited me as I made my ascent up the seemingly endless, pitch-black stairwell.

As I pushed open the door at the top of the stairs, I made sure to step out quickly to avoid getting jumped in the doorway. Standing about five yards from the front door was the punk that scuffed my shoes wearing a white t-shirt. Unfortunately for me, however, there were several other guys standing behind him, also wearing white t-shirts. At about the same time, I realized that there were two fully capable guys from my unit down there in the bar sitting with my girlfriend, and they think I'm still in the bathroom.

Once again, I was presented with some choices. With my feet propped up while typing this, I can see that there were a ton of possible options looking back. In the intensity of that moment, however, I distinctly remember only two options that went through my head.

Option A: I could run my mouth a little bit and then try to get my boys. I guess it depended on how fast I could get down the stairs and whether they would start hitting me as soon as I turned my back. Then I thought about a time I had seen another guy get jumped in that dark stairwell by a few other guys, and it did not go well for him. The thought of falling down the stairs and subsequently getting stomped out by four dudes did not sound very appealing.

Option B: Preemptive strike. I could hit the punk in the mouth for disrespecting me in public and scuffing up the shoes Mama got me for Christmas. I figured we could just see how it goes from there, but I knew dang good and well that I wasn't going to wuss out and get my butt kicked like I did freshman year.

So, I went with Option B. Before the guy could even swing, I dropped him like a sack of potatoes. In my opponent's descent, two of his friends were knocked off balance falling like bowling pins onto the street. I had no problem with them. I just wanted retribution against the punk that offended me. So I jumped on top of him to give him a few more to make sure I got my point across. I could feel myself getting hit, but I was so drunk that I could not tell exactly who was hitting me. Then I saw it.

It was a tree. Not a lumber making, grow out of the ground type of tree. It was the tree on the label of a Timberland boot. It was kind of like a dream. You know, when everything is in slow motion. You can't seem to do anything fast, and your body is stuck in sloth mode. It was like that. I saw it coming but I could not move or put my hands up.

Boom! The boot made direct contact on my nose and upper lip. I had gotten blasted like a perfect punt on fourth down to pin the enemy deep in their own territory. My head shot upwards as the red mist of blood and spit flew into the streetlight illuminated night sky. My entire body fell back into the hurdler stretch position. I am not sure if I got knocked out for a brief second or not, but I was rocked. I jumped up and pushed one guy and started to fight with another when it all broke up. Looking back, they probably just did not want my blood all over them. I probably looked like a zombie, wasted on booze, punch drunk, and bleeding out of my nose and mouth. Pretty gross.

Then I see my battle buddy from basic training standing there eating a donor kebab. So I cussed him out for not jumping in. Then my girlfriend comes out to check on me with genuine concern in her eyes, and I cuss her out because she was not there—or some other irrational excuse to cuss her out. I saw the flashing lights coming. Time to go!

Is this a Christian? Is this what a follower of Christ would do? How many times could this have been avoided? Would Jesus strike someone in the face over some scuffed shoes?
I was lost, but I did not know it. It said Christian on my dog tag, but was I really with Christ? I think that I treated Jesus' sacrifice on the Cross as a flu shot that would give me immunity from eternal damnation so I could just live however I wanted.

It was always someone else's fault anyway. If he hadn't stepped on my shoe; then we would have had no problem. If he had not stared at me and taunted me from across the room, there never would have been a fight anyway. I think all of us have the incredible ability to blame other people for our problems—to justify and rationalize away our own actions, somehow, someway.

Even if I did admit that in my heart, I wanted someone to test me; I wanted that fight to happen; I wanted the reputation of a tough guy; I enjoyed it. I could still blame it on someone else. If my dad wasn't so mean, or if I never got bullied, or if my girlfriend hadn't cheated on me, then maybe I would not have so much anger. Maybe this would never have happened? To be honest, there is some truth to this. The truth is that sin has consequences that go beyond us. Our actions affect others. What is over for us in a moment, something that we are rationalizing away and ducking accountability for, is

33

potentially going to affect someone else for a long time. Sin makes us a slave—sins of others and sins of our own.

Another thing that would have changed the situation would have been if I were actively following Christ. If I were reading my Bible, praying, and trying to live as a disciple of Christ in the company of others who were doing the same, it would all have been different. That's the thing about being lost; you're working for the enemy and don't even know it.

Jesus said, "Whoever is not with me is against me, and whoever does not gather with me scatters." (Matthew 12:30 NIV) In his letter to the Philippians, the Apostle Paul wrote, "For, as I have often told you before and now tell you again even with tears, many live as enemies of the cross of Christ. Their destiny is destruction, their god is their stomach, and their glory is in their shame." (3:18-19)

My first deployment in Iraq was right around the corner. I was going to need God more than ever in my life, and yet my actions indicated that I wanted nothing to do with Him. If anything, I lived as an enemy of God. The bad wolf was winning, as I drifted further into my own yearning for pleasure and violence. The good wolf was struggling to find crumbs. What would happen if the good wolf died? What if I were too far gone to save?

Chapter 8
Hopeless

In July of 2004, most of the other folks my age were enjoying summer vacation from their first year of college, or perhaps, they were just working to make enough money to party the summer away, worried about exactly nothing. I was several months into a pretty rough deployment in Iraq as an eighteen-year-old Army private. We had been shot at a few times, hit a few IEDs (Improvised Explosive Devices), and taken some mortars—all that fun stuff. A lot of the other platoons saw significantly more combat than we did, but a lot had happened since we left the snowy streets of Germany behind on Valentine's Day. It was possible that I may have already killed some enemy combatants, but there was no way to know for sure. I was no longer green; that's for certain.

There had been some car bombs that had successfully hit several targets in and around the city. One was horribly vicious, as many Iraqis were killed when someone detonated a bus full of mortars. My buddy from basic actually got a bronze star with valor device for shooting up one car bomb that was attempting to take out the commander of our unit. We had received a ton of training on how to identify and deal with Vehicle Borne Improvised Explosive Devices (VBIEDs).

It came out of nowhere. There was a dirt driveway over to the left, but I did not see a car when we passed by. I have no idea to be honest, but the first time I saw it was when it flew past our Humvee in a cloud of dust. I was in the gunners hatch as always, and I immediately started to ask my Truck Commander what to do. The car went up behind the truck we were pulling security for on the way back to our base. I was in a panic, and honestly felt that the vehicle would explode at any minute and blow me in half.

Everything about that car matched the characteristics of suspicious vehicles that I had been trained to be on the lookout for.

It had tinted windows, was weighed down in the back, and was driving erratically and aggressively. I yelled and waved, hoping that the driver would pull to the side of the road without incident. With no response, I fired some warning shots to the side of the vehicle. Still there was no attempt to stop or move out of the way. They were getting really close to our other truck, and I thought they were going to detonate on them. I was the only one who could do anything. I opened fire on the vehicle.

I continued to fire until the vehicle stopped. Through the shot-out windows I saw the carnage inside as we passed by on the driver's side of the vehicle. There were three men inside, all of them shot. I knew that one of them was already dead. I saw him slumped over in the back seat with a hole in his head. My heart sank inside my chest as we pulled to the front of the convoy to pick up security while the medic rendered aid to the wounded.

I was praying—praying that they would find explosives or weapons, anything that would make this all right. I can remember tears coming to my eyes as I listened intently to the radio for a situation report from the party on the scene. Then I heard the news I hoped I would not hear. No weapons, no explosives, one guy is dead, and the other two don't look good. What had I done?

Remember how I asked if you were a good person? If you were to ask me that question, even in the aftermath of the New Year's Eve festivities, I would have said, "Yeah, I guess." I mean, what is the standard of goodness anyways? I knew I had done some messed up stuff, but I could think of lots of people worse than me. That was all over now. I was now the worst person I knew. I had taken the lives of innocent people.

As soon as we got back to the base, the investigation of the day's events began. I was a wreck. I was just a small-town kid who thought he was a thug, who wanted everybody to think he was harder than he really was. Not even nineteen years old yet, I could not help but think that I might have to spend the best years of my life in a military prison. The situation continued to replay in my mind over and over again as we walked into the battalion headquarters.

The driver, TC, platoon sergeant, platoon leader, company commander, and I sat down at a big table in the operations center. The colonel came in and started to get each person's accounts of the events. Some agreed with my decision to engage; others did not. I gave my account and started to break down as I described the events and the motivations for my actions. I had done everything that I was trained to do, but yet there I was with innocent blood on my hands. The colonel then asked me, "Did you feel threatened? Did you think that car was going to blow up? Did you feel like other soldier's lives were in danger?" I truthfully answered affirmatively to each of those questions. After determining that my actions were in accordance with the rules of engagement and escalation of force protocols, it was all over. Nothing was ever said of it again.

Even though I had been justified in the eyes of men, I could not stop myself from thinking about where I stood in the eyes of God. How could I come back from this? How could God still love me? There was no way I could be forgiven for what I had done. There was no way I could make it right. Even if I gave my life, it would only pay the debt for one of the men I had killed. I had a debt I could not pay.

Before that day, I could always rationalize my issues away and justify my actions. I could avoid the guilt and responsibility that accompanied my decisions. I tried to, of course, but that time it did not work. *It was the driver of the vehicle's fault. What was he thinking? Everybody knows that you don't just jump into an American convoy, mainly, because something like this would happen.* But this would mean that I had executed people for either poor driving or ignorance, and that did not make me feel much better.

You know what? I know who to blame. It was God's fault. He is supposed to be in charge of this whole mess down here, and if He did not arrange it, He certainly let it happen. But there was a problem. No matter how I tried to rationalize it; it was I who pulled that trigger. I had a choice. If I had not pulled the trigger each of those men would have gone on with their day, back to their families, or wherever they were headed that evening. God did not pull the trigger, I did. This broke me.

A couple of months later, I went home on R&R: a brief leave of absence in the middle of the deployment. People were there to greet us in droves at the Atlanta airport, to shake our hands, and to thank us for our valiant service. I could not even look them in the eye. I just wanted to find my way to the next terminal so I could catch my connecting flight. The plane landed at the local airport back home. I tried to hold my head up high as I saw my mama and little brother waiting down the corridor near the baggage claim. The emotions started to build the closer I got to her.

When we got within arm's reach of each other, I stopped. I did not know what to do next. I could not speak because of the tears welling up inside me. I wondered if she knew what I had done, if her baby boy was a killer. Could she tell by looking at me that a part of me had died over there? I fell into her arms and sobbed. Everything came out, all of the emotions that I had kept penned up inside of me so I could keep it together and do my job. Mama was crying, too, as I am sure she perceived that whatever I had been through over there was just too much for me to handle. I am not sure how long we stood there sobbing, but it felt as if hours went by, or perhaps the whole world had stopped turning all together.

Chapter 9
Darkness

Now that I had already committed what I saw as such a horrible sin, what was the use in trying to be a good person? I mean, when you have killed people, does the little stuff really even matter anymore? I think that is the way sinning was for me in my head. Even from early on, I had a faulty way of thinking about what sin is, who God is, and the way that we relate to those things. When I was a kid, I figured that sin was bad and that if I did it that maybe I would get struck by lightning or some terrible Old Testament plague would fall upon me. But when I saw other people sin, nothing happened—no lightning, fire from heaven, hailstorms, or any of that stuff. In fact, they seemed to prosper from their wickedness and wrongdoing.

This observation led me to try the things I was told were wrong. And once you've done it, why stop? My thinking was, well you're already guilty of breaking the law, why not keep breaking it if there appear to be no consequences? This type of thinking is extremely dangerous, and it took me to some deeply dark places.

It goes like this; perhaps you are familiar with it. Well I've already smoked cigarettes, so I might as well drink. Well I've already had sex; I'm not pure anymore, so why not just hook up with whoever I want? Well I've taken other pills, so why not try these? Or, in my case, well I've already killed other human beings, along with everything under that on the totem pole of sinfulness, so who cares?

You know who some of the most dangerous people on earth are? Criminals that are out on bail and are awaiting trial. They know that very soon the gavel is going to fall and the judge will sentence them to a prison cell for possibly the rest of their natural lives for a crime that they have already committed. They have nothing to lose; they are already condemned.

With a person like that, anything is possible, because a point has been reached when the consequences that govern normal decision making no longer matter. I think that many who do not know God think very wrongly about His nature and drastically underestimate the sacrifice of Jesus on the Cross. After the car incident, I felt like God could not possibly love me, that no one could really love me, and that this was just a dark world where people use each other as means to selfish ends. In my mind, Heaven was out of the picture. Either I would cease to exist whenever my heart stopped beating, or I would go to hell and be punished for the things I had done.

Between the years of 2004 and 2008, I lived a life of lust and violence. I lived completely for myself in every way shape and fashion. In the midst of my chasing after pleasure and cheap thrills, I hurt a lot of people in word and deed. Please forgive me. I am so sorry. I am not the same person I was back then, and I pray that the Lord would heal up any wounds that I inflicted on you.

They say that darkness itself is not really a thing, but instead, it is the absence of light. For instance, check out the difference between a new moon and a full moon. The more light is removed, the deeper that darkness becomes. Jesus was big on talking about light and darkness (See Matthew 6:23 and John's Gospel). There are many spiritual parallels and metaphors dealing with the two. I could feel that there was something missing inside of me, and I tried to fill it with anything that would make me feel different. In the process, I moved further and further away from what would really satisfy and bring me lasting peace.

I heard a quote from Jim Carey one time that said, "I wish that everybody could be rich and famous and do everything they ever wanted to do, so that they could see it's not the answer." I did it. I lived the life I wanted. I did whatever I wanted to do, whenever I wanted to do it. Yet, at the end of the high, the drunk, the sex, the fight, or whatever else you want to add in, there was still that emptiness.

40

The first time I came across the book of Ecclesiastes, I thought that it was the most depressing thing I had ever read, but the more I thought about it, the more I identified with King Solomon. In Chapter 2, Solomon talks about how he "denied his eyes nothing they desired and refused his heart no pleasure" (2:10). In the end of it all—and this guy had it all—these things were vanity and meaninglessness; they brought no lasting peace.

Oh, how I searched in the dark for something that would make me feel good again. It's like a person coming into a pitch-black house that they are not familiar with. They walk around combing the walls looking for the light switch that must be somewhere. In the midst of time, they grope every object that they find along the wall. Pictures get knocked down. Toys get stepped on. Toes get stubbed. It is not until they turn on the light that they see all of chaos and carnage in their wake. I'm going to hit you with a few Bible verses right here that I would like for you to think about as we move forward with the story.

"Your word is a lamp for my feet, a light on my path." (Psalm 119:105 NIV)

"This is the verdict: Light has come into the world, but people loved darkness instead of light because their deeds were evil." (John 3:19 NIV)

"When Jesus spoke again to the people, he said, "I am the light of the world. Whoever follows me will never walk in darkness but will have the light of life." (John 8:12 NIV)

"This is the message we have heard from him and declare to you: God is light; in him there is no darkness at all. If we claim to have fellowship with him and yet walk in the darkness, we lie and do not live out the truth. But if we walk in the light, as he is in the light, we have fellowship with one another, and the blood of Jesus, his Son, purifies us from all sin." (1 John 1: 5-9 NIV)

Chapter 10
Trees

Christianity is not a flu shot—an immunization from condemnation. It is not fire insurance to keep you from burning in hell. Plain and simple, if people have known you for a while, and they do not know that you are a follower of Jesus Christ, then you probably aren't. Jesus said that a person would know a tree by its fruit in Chapter 7 of Matthew's Gospel. The Lord polarized it by simply stating that trees produce fruit of their kind; a bad tree produces fruit of evil, and a good tree produces good fruit. Then there was the tree that produced no fruit, which Jesus cursed. Jesus also said that trees that do not produce good fruit are cut down and thrown into the fire. Of course, with some in-depth Bible study, one can deduce that the Lord is primarily and prophetically speaking about the nation of Israel in these circumstances. However, these principles are still applicable for the unfruitful Christian.

For instance, James—Jesus' brother—wrote about this issue of fruit being the evidence of our identity as believers. Keep in mind that He wrote this to mainly new Jewish Christians within the First Century Church. "Show me your faith without deeds, and I will show you my faith by my deeds. You believe that there is one God. Good! Even the demons believe that—and shudder." (James 2:18-19 NIV) That's saying a lot right there. I think about the fact that a person simply believing in the existence of God is not enough. It's a start, but it is not nearly enough. This is one of the toughest parts about living in an increasingly secular, post-Christian, society. Because there are so many non-believers, those who do believe in God can think that just acknowledging the existence of the Creator is sufficient for salvation. The devil knows that God exists too; is he any less condemned?

This reminds me of a conversation I had while preparing for my second deployment. Specifically, it reminds me of "The

Scientist." They named a combat outpost after him. I did not know him very well. We were not close. We were only in the same platoon for a few months, but The Scientist is still on my mind today.

T-bird, The Scientist, and I ended up in the same room together, cleaning weapons while the rest of the platoon was doing something else during the field training exercises in the deserts of New Mexico. Somehow, God came into the conversation, and we soon discovered that The Scientist was an atheist. I think it was the first time I had ever heard anyone say out loud that they did not believe in God.

T-bird was quick to rebuke him jokingly by reminding him that we would all be going to Iraq soon, and it might not be a good time to be messing around with God. He began to defend his doubts from a scientific and philosophic perspective, thus earning his nickname. Then there was the typical "you can't prove or disprove God conversation." But after that, it became biblical, as The Scientist began to ask me about things from scripture and presented issues that he had with the Bible, church history, and Christians in general. I had nothing in response to his comments. It ended with a "coexist" bumper sticker, metaphorically of course, as we decided to respectfully disagree with one another. Even though neither party conceded, the debate was clearly won by The Scientist. It turned out that an atheist knew the Bible better than I did.

I wonder if the conversation would have been different if I had known that The Scientist would be killed in Iraq the following year. God put me in the right place at the right time to make an impact in the life of another person, and I failed. I was apathetic toward the whole situation, much like most of the people I see today. The Creator of the universe loved crappy people like you and me so much that He became one of us, died to show His love for us, and we do not even tell anybody.

It reminds me of a quote by performer, magician, and atheist, Penn Gillette. He said, "If you believe that there's a heaven and a hell, and people could be going to hell or not getting eternal life, and you think that it's not really worth telling them this because it would make it socially awkward. How much do you have to hate somebody to believe everlasting life is possible and not tell them that?" Although I do not look back often and wish I could change things because I realize that my past is what made me who I am today, I do want that conversation back.

If you call yourself a Christian, then you have been given the task of making disciples for Christ, not sitting on your butt and waiting to go to heaven. If you profess to believe that Jesus of Nazareth really was God walking around in human flesh, that He consciously chose to be killed for your sins, and that He actually came back to life after being dead for a while, then this belief should be the focal point of your entire life. That should change you. I did not live like I really believed that, or maybe I just took it for granted. In reality, I was a tree that bore no fruit for God's glory, calling myself a Christian, yet living completely apart from God.

Perhaps if I had read my Bible, I might have had the answers for The Scientist. The thought of Him being separated from God for all of eternity really freaks me out. I pray that somehow outside of space, time, and matter, in the realm of the spiritual things, that young man will get an opportunity to see his Creator face to face. In that time, it is my hope, that having been convinced of His existence, The Scientist will bow his knee and accept His Lordship and sacrifice. "Jesus looked at them and said, 'With man this is impossible, but with God all things are possible.'" (Matthew 19:26)

However, I also see other verses in the Word of God that point to the urgency of salvation: "And as it is appointed unto men once to die, but after this the judgment." (Hebrews 9:27 KJV) Perhaps he recalled the conversation we had, put together the pieces, realized the truth, and trusted the Lord for salvation before he died. These unknowns have haunted me.

Chapter 11
Death

I learned a good bit about death during my second deployment to Iraq. After unrealistically vowing to eliminate the insurgents that killed The Scientist and Binky, we actually got the opportunity get some payback in the same area as their fatal blast.

We were on a small kill-team mission. After walking a few miles in the dark, we implanted in this empty gas station a couple of hundred yards from an abandoned checkpoint where the enemy liked to emplace roadside bombs. After spending most of the day inside the house, we determined that we would spend the last few hours before dark up on the rooftop.

As the First Sergeant's patrol went through the checkpoint and past our location, we could see a kid talking on a cell phone or some type of communication device across the river. This may not seem strange to Americans, but it's pretty weird for 2007 Iraq. After that we were on high alert. I was watching the sector to the south, and I spotted two guys walking down from the village at the top of the hill about a half a mile away. They got into a car and started heading in our direction. I alerted my sniper. "Hud! We got a possible." Like in spades.

Sure enough, the vehicle stopped in the checkpoint right over the top of a crater from a previously detonated IED. Our chief was messing with the radios in attempt to communicate with the leadership at the combat outpost. Two guys got out of the car and walked to the trunk. As soon as they opened it, we spotted the propane tank. They loved using propane tanks like you grill with and those big acetylene tanks you see at welding shops. We were waiting for clearance to fire, but the radios were acting stupid. Hud popped up to a knee to make sure he had positive identification and a clear shot. When he moved to a kneeling position from the prone, Hud lost his defilade, and one of the emplacers saw him.

They quickly scrambled to get back in the car. Then Hud made one of the best shots I've ever seen. The driver was just pulling off when Hud popped him right at the base of his neck. The car flipped over on one of the jersey barriers, and I came across the building with the 249 SAW (Squad Automatic Weapon). The two guys in the backseat that I had seen come down the hill from the town squirted out of the upside-down car as we engaged it. They both fell several times as they continued to try to escape, only to run into more of my automatic weapon fire. I was told later that they were found dead near the river, each with multiple gunshot wounds and $150 US currency in their pockets.

We were elated. We had done our jobs. We had finally gotten the SOBs that were planting the IEDs on the road to the Combat Out Post. This time was so much different than the car incident. I had killed two men, snuffed them out, and I could not have been happier. This was good. Right?

Then there was the time the other small kill team from our platoon engaged some suspected emplacers on one of the main roads in our area of operation. We pulled on to the scene pretty quickly after the firing had stopped. I was not there to witness the actual engagement, and I do not know how it all went down, but when we pulled up there was a guy that was already quite dead and a couple of others that were shot up pretty badly. We pulled up next to one of the casualties, and Hud jumped out to start working on him. He had taken the advanced combat life saver course and was just as good as a medic, probably better than some. From the gunner's hatch, I watched as Hud did everything he could to save this guy's life.

Because we were not there to see how it happened, we did not get a chance to see them as the enemy that day; instead we just saw human beings dying on the hot desert sand. It broke my heart to see Hud try unendingly, and in vain, to get this guy's lung back in his chest. I told him that he should just stop working on the poor fellow, as there was no hope. But he refused. He was not going to quit until the very end. Just before the guy died, I saw something in his eyes. It was something that I had never seen before; a type of fear that I had not previously witnessed or experienced. He had seen something, or felt something, something bad, and then the light faded from his eyes.

I started to think about the men that I had killed a few weeks earlier. Is this the way they died? Were they just normal, young guys that you can find all over the good ole USA, who were trying to make a buck? $150 US is no small change in Iraq, especially for one day of work—think of a year's salary. I can remember having a briefcase in my hands for some public relations project that had thirty-two million Iraqi dinar in it. It wouldn't even buy you a new car in the States. To think that I was so happy to kill them makes me sick. Especially when I picture the families that they left behind.

I got to see that side of it on our end; it made me hate even harder. "Doc" was our medic. He had gotten traded to another platoon later in the deployment, but he was always our medic. An IED hit the very first route clearance mission we rolled out on. Doc was riding in my truck that night. I was in the gunner's hatch. I ducked down as we passed by it to brace for the impact. It detonated right behind Doc's door in the rear driver's side passenger seat. It knocked my 240Bravo Machine Gun off the spindle mount and rung my bell pretty good, but Doc took the brunt of the lick. He got his hip banged up a little, but other than that, we were all fine. The truck, on the other hand, had four flat tires and was leaking fuel all over the street.

I had been hit a few times during my first tour, so I was not really shaken up too badly. Tido, our driver, decided to start smoking cigarettes again! LOL. Doc appeared to be troubled, which surprised me because he was an experienced sergeant who had already been deployed a few times before he got to our unit. He looked me in my eyes and told me that he had a feeling he was not going to make it home. I shook it off and told Doc to "shut up with that negative bull****," and reminded him that it was early on, and we didn't need to be thinking like that.

47

Unfortunately, Doc's premonition was accurate. I'll never forget the feeling of dread and helplessness I felt as we watched the smoke rising from across the river. We heard the explosion, but there were explosions all the time, usually controlled detonations of IED's that had been found. Then somebody ran out of the radio room at the COP and said, "Third platoon got hit. There are casualties. I think there might be KIA's." Dead American boys, thousands of miles away from home, would only be henceforth known by pictures and memories.

Doc was only one of three men that were killed in action that day. The other two were just kids like me, Pac and Lope. I knew them fairly well, but not like I knew Doc. I considered Doc a legitimate friend. We had eaten meals together, drank from each other's cups, slept in the same vehicle in the field. I hated whoever did this. I hated. We went on a raid for the guys who were suspected of making and setting up the IED that night. We got 'em. It did nothing to ease the pain. None of us felt any better. Maybe worse.

When I got back from that tour, I went straight to the barracks and started to get wasted, just as I had done the deployment before. At some point in the night, a kid I had never seen walked into the room with some buddies of mine. They yelled out, "This is Doc's kid!" Many of us broke down thinking about how we failed to bring his daddy home. I think he was the oldest of four or five kids that Doc left behind. He proudly, through tears, announced to us that he was going to be a marine once he finished his senior year of high school. He wanted to go kill the SOBs that killed his daddy.

How many people are running around mad at the world, mad at God, because I killed their daddy, or brother, or best friend?

"What benefit did you reap at that time from the things you are now ashamed of? Those things result in death!" (Romans 6:21)

Chapter 12
Rain

I am convinced that rain is the most taken for granted blessing in this world. We need water to survive; yet we whine about a rainy day. I did not really appreciate the rain until my first tour in Iraq. Like I said, we got there in February and I went on R&R in September. In that seven-month period, I did not see one drop of rain. Every day it was like the sun was following me around, hovering a few feet above me with a hair dryer. Once I got back to Carolina, I could not wait for it to rain. Once it did, I stripped down to my skivvies and went out to dance in it. I felt like the dude in the movie *Shawshank Redemption*.

Jesus said, "He causes his sun to rise on the evil and the good and sends rain on the righteous and the unrighteous." (Matthew 5:45) It is not my intention to paint the picture that when a person is living a life apart from God that it is all misery and bitterness, that nothing good ever happens. That would be highly inaccurate. As the verse above would indicate, our merciful God blesses both those who love Him and those who don't. I think that the main difference is what people do with those blessings, how they play the cards they're dealt. Do they dance in the rain? Or complain about it and curse the clouds that brought the weather?

It was in this time, living apart from God, that some of my closest bonds of friendship were formed with the boys in the Hoodang Clan. That was the nickname for our platoon my second tour. The year 2007 was one of the best years of my life, mainly because of the people that I shared it with. Sure, there were lots of crappy moments; it's Iraq, but overall, I had some great laughs and good times with people I still love dearly over a decade later. It was also in this time period that I received the greatest blessing that a man can ever hope for: a loyal, loving, and supportive wife.

49

We were introduced to each other through the wife of one of my Army buddies. This relationship was different than any other relationship I had before. All of my previous relationships were mainly about what I could get out of them. I liked having a pretty girl on my arm to show off like a trophy. To be honest, I liked having a girl around to have sex with whenever I wanted instead of having to go through the trouble of trying to hook up with a different girl every night at the club—too expensive, drinks ain't cheap. Most of the time, I would be with a girl for a couple of weeks, and then, before I got too attached, I would find some way to wiggle out of it.

When wifey and I started out, there were 6,000 miles between us. I was a bit of a night owl and loved to hit the gym around midnight. As some of you will be familiar, there is nothing more frustrating for a gym rat than to have to wait for a bench press or some other piece of equipment instrumental to that day's workout. But at midnight, the gym is a ghost town and you can pretty much have free reign of the place. After my workout, I would go to the Internet café or smelly room full of computers. I would check Myspace and emails, but the main reason I was there was to talk on Instant Messenger with this cute little blond bunny rabbit from the Midwest. She was my little taste of home; I loved her, and I had never even met her.

Once again, I made it home from deployment with all my parts and a pocket full of money. I asked her if she would be my woman on the phone one night, and by the next day, I had booked her a flight to El Paso, TX where I was stationed. It was amazing. I had never been so happy. She got my name tattooed on her butt three days after she met me. She was the one.

After spending a week together—about the best week ever, from what I can remember—we went our separate ways. She flew back to Illinois, and I drove to Carolina for a couple of weeks of leave. I could not get her off my mind; I was smitten. There were a few days left in my post-deployment block leave before I needed to report back to my unit, and I decided that I could not live without her. I was going to drive all night from North Carolina to Northern Illinois, through Chicago in a blizzard, and that little nineteen-year-old bunny rabbit was coming back to Texas with me.

Those first couple of months were filled with blissful adventure. We were engaged on Valentine's Day and married a month later at the Justice of the Peace. With the company of a few friends as witnesses and Ring Pops for wedding bands, we were pronounced husband and wife. Life was good. But then the excitement began to wear off as the mundane drudgery of everyday life began to reveal itself. I was usually gone from before sunrise until after dusk. She was stuck in our one-bedroom apartment all of the time. Looking back, it must have been hard for a girl fresh out of high school that had never really spent any substantial time on her own. She was away from home and living in a new place. Perhaps because we were so in love, we thought that it would always be unicorns and rainbows, but that was not the case.

You see, we are all broken in some way, shape, or fashion. Some of us are more broken than others, without a doubt, but we are all damaged from the fallen world in which we find ourselves. Our sins, and the sins others have committed against us, leave emotional and spiritual scars. As you will find out later in the story, I am covered in visible scars. Upon first meeting me, you probably would not notice them, but after a little while they will start to grab your attention. Each of them has its own story, its own pain. The emotional and spiritual wounds of my wife and me were not apparent to each other in the first few months. Infatuation has a way of blinding us and keeping us from seeing the imperfections that are always there just beneath the surface.

We both brought baggage into the relationship. It's kind of like a vacation. When you first get to the beach getaway, or vacation destination of your choice, you throw the bags in the corner of the room and go out to have fun. Then after the first few swimming trips, changing to go out to dinner, digging through the bags to find the

51

shoes that you know you packed but can't seem to dig out, next thing you know, the baggage is all over the place. It was that way with us.

We both brought in the baggage from failed and unhealthy relationships from our past. I had justifiable trust issues from the girl who broke my heart, the failed engagement that I did not even mention prior to my second deployment, my parents' awful relationship, and the many untrustworthy women I had known over the years. I also had my volatile temper, the emotional damage from my two prior deployments, and misconceptions about marriage and life in general. She had different issues but issues just the same. I thrived in confrontation; she would shut down and withdraw from it. When we fought, as we often did, nothing productive would come from it. Instead of solving problems, we mainly just wounded each other with hurtful words and unnecessary jabs.

I had been blessed from above with a beautiful wife, a good job, friends, a nice car, and everything that I needed, but I was not the man I should have been. It was all taken for granted and poisoned by my selfish pride and the dark spots on my soul. If you are not the right person yourself, then nobody will ever be the right person for you. If you are a selfish jerk filled with bitterness, anger, and resentment, then you will ruin any blessing that God gives you. Jesus said, "Neither do people pour new wine into old wineskins. If they do, the skins will burst; the wine will run out and the wineskins will be ruined. No, they pour new wine into new wineskins, and both are preserved." (Matthew 9:17)

If it had not been for God's intervention, I would have completely destroyed and abandoned our marriage. The thought of it makes me shudder. Hang on to your seats folks, this is when the story gets crazy.

Chapter 13
God Showed Up

Remember that part in the movie, *Forrest Gump*, when Lieutenant Dan is asking, "Where the hell is this God of yours?" Then a hurricane comes out of nowhere, and Forrest says, "Right about then, God showed up." He was there all along, but I didn't really notice. He had kept me safe through two tours in Iraq and arranged so many things, but I only realized it in hindsight through the eyes of faith. For me, it would not be a hurricane, but instead, it all started with lightning.

Wifey and I were on the way back to Carolina for our church wedding. For those of you who are familiar, in the Army you get a housing allowance when you are married, but single soldiers do not get this substantial amount of monthly income. This is why we got married at the Justice of the Peace. Otherwise, I couldn't afford to keep her. Just kidding. Kinda. But I did want her to be able to have a real wedding with the dress, her family, cake, and all the rest. I also hoped that this vacation time and all of the attached excitement with the wedding would help to improve our relationship, which was growing more and more unhappy.

It was July, and we were driving from El Paso to North Carolina taking the interstate 10, 20, 30, 40 route. By the way, the air conditioning in my mustang was broken. Fellas, if you ever find a woman that will drive across the entire state of Texas in July with no air conditioning without killing you, then you have found yourself a "keeper." We were not planning on stopping, as we just wanted to get that miserable twenty-four-hour drive over with as quickly as possible. Then about thirty minutes west of Texarkana, we got caught in a pretty stout thunderstorm. There was lightning flashing all around us, and then my car died. We were so pissed. We had been driving all day in that cramped car with our little dog, in the hot sun, and now what? I did not have the time or money to be dealing with this crap.

We were able to get a tow truck out there after a while, and he pulled us into Texarkana. As fate would have it, none of the service stations were open because of the 4th of July holiday. We would have to stay the night in one of the area's finest establishments until a mechanic could get to it in the morning. I think it was a Motel 8 that allowed pets.

Well, our travels were not going according to plan, but we figured that we would make the best of a lousy situation. We went out to a local bar and dance club right across the street. Drinks were flowing, and after having a good time dancing vertically, we returned to the motel to do some horizontal dancing.

The next morning we were summoned down to the repair shop where my vehicle was being checked out. I was sweating bullets thinking that I was going to be the recipient of some bad news. I figured that whatever was wrong with my vehicle was going to be too expensive for me to cover. We had a wedding to get ready for in North Carolina, and being stuck in Texarkana waiting for parts I could not pay for did not seem like it was going to be very fun.

Strangely enough, good news was waiting on us. My car was ready to go. Already?! Apparently, my car had been hit by lightning, and it blew out all the fuses in my fuse box. They even went ahead and put some coolant in my air conditioner, for which my wife and I were quite thankful.

The wedding was lovely. She was lovely. I had never been so proud. In that moment, she was the most beautiful woman I had ever seen. This time in Carolina was really nice, but the time came for us to head on back to good ole West Texas.

Unfortunately, the dynamic of our relationship settled back into the same funk we had been in before the wedding. After about a month of being back in El Paso, I started to seriously consider that our marriage might have been a mistake. In fact, I was in the middle of an IED defeat course thinking that I might go check with the JAG office during lunch to see what I would be looking at legally if I decided to file for an annulment or divorce. There seemed to be no hope. We were fighting all the time, and I was going to be in Iraq again next year anyway. If we were going to end it, then it might as well be now, before we had too much invested.

Then I got a text message from my wife telling me to call her when I got out of class. With a "what now?" attitude and accompanying tone, I gave her a ring, still planning on seeing a lawyer during lunch. She asked if I could go pick up some pregnancy tests on my way home. Talk about a game changer! Instead of going to the JAG office on my lunch break, I went to the Walgreen's pharmacy. She was right. I was going to be a dad. How's that for timing?

By the way, if that was not cool enough, guess when wifey got pregnant? That's right folks, Texarkana. We were going to have a lightning baby!

The Boo Boo Bear, as she is affectionately known in our house, changed everything for me. It was Easter Sunday, and instead of being at church, we were at William Beaumont Army Medical Center. If I am not mistaken, I remember being really tired because I was at a friend's house late playing video games the night before. Husband of the year, right? She started having contractions really early in the morning so I only had a couple of hours of sleep. I had no clue what was going on, being a first-time father, and I had no idea what to expect. I like to think that I was at least a good cheerleader. I was scared, but I tried not to show it. At some point later on in her labor something happened.

Everything was going smoothly, she was dilating well, and there seemed to be no concerns for baby or mother. Then, for no apparent reason, the baby's pulse started to drop. At first, I thought that maybe there was a problem with the heart monitor. It's just a patch on an elastic belt that goes around the mother's stomach, not super high tech. Sometimes it moves around and loses the signal. Then the alarms started going off, and the panic really set in.

55

All of the other times that I had been scared in Iraq, it was different. I had a machine gun, brothers at arms, armored vehicles; I was not invincible, but certainly far from helpless. This was different. There was nothing that I could do. I prayed. The nurses and doctor came running in as the lights blinked and alarms blared. All I could do was stay out of the way praying and crying. There was a feeling that my sins had come to revisit me, and that it was time for me to pay the piper.

No, No, No, please don't take her. I said it over and over again. *Take me. Kill me right now. But let her live. I deserve to die for the things I have done, but please don't take her.* This was my prayer over and over again. It was the first time I really prayed in my whole life; I think. Sure, I had said many prayers in my life, but none like this. God had to hear me. I know He heard me! He was the only one who could help.

As the medical folks continued to try to reposition my wife and get her ready for a potential C-section if necessary, I continued to pray. The harder I prayed, the more the pulse would rise, and when I stopped, it would start to go back down again. It was wild. It was the first time I can remember feeling like God actually heard my prayers, and I saw Him answer. Things would eventually stabilize, and that Easter Sunday my wife gave birth to a beautiful, healthy, baby girl. New Life.

God was busy that day, as you will find out a little later in the story. But I did not have time to get right with Him then, even though He had really done me a solid by sparing my daughter's life. I had to get ready to deploy once again to Iraq in a month. Only this time I had something to lose.

Chapter 14
Best Worst Day Ever!

This part of the story, I have told so many times to people all over the place. It is the part that I have looked forward to, and also dreaded, the most. Though I have talked about this day with more people than probably any other subject in my life, how do I tell it when it's official? How do I put it on paper? To be honest, in my prayers for this book, it is this part that I picture the reader being impacted by the most. When I think about you reading this book, it is in this chapter that I see you in my mind, whoever you are. Lord, do your thing. Please.

It was the first time I had someone there to say goodbye to. Wifey, her mother (love you Pamma), and our little Boo Boo Bear were with me basically all day as I dropped off bags, drew weapons, and did the rest of the day of deployment stuff. My group was flying out that day, exactly one month after the birth of our daughter. The rest of my platoon was already in the Kuwait staging area. I'm extremely grateful that my chain of command allowed me to fly out on one of the later flights so that I could spend at least a little time with my new family.

After all of the business was handled, everyone gathered in the gymnasium down near the airfield. Soaking in those last few moments together, there was a feeling inside me that I had not experienced in my two prior deployments. I didn't want to go. I didn't want to stop holding my daughter. I wanted that hug with my wife to last forever. I hoped for a brief moment that the bus would just pull away without me, and long after the last person left, the lights in the gym would shut off, and we would still be there holding each other. Thoughts that I did not dare let become words were racing through my head, as the time seemed to fast-forward in slow motion. Would this be the last time I would hold my daughter? Would she grow up without her daddy? Would I only be a folded-

57

up flag and a picture on the wall to my wife after today? Would she be a widow before she could even buy a beer?

As a staff sergeant and an experienced combat veteran with two deployments under my belt, I tried to keep my composure. Stoic. The first timers and young guys are always looking to the more seasoned leaders to see how they should feel. I did on my first trip. I had a bad feeling about this one. I wondered if this was what Doc was talking about. I wondered if he felt this way as he said goodbye to his wife and kids for the last time.

They say, "Third time's a charm." I disagree. This deployment was pretty crappy. We lived in crowded tents with poorly performing air conditioning. The only real threat was from sporadic and usually inaccurate rocket attacks. The missions were pretty lame, not like my previous deployments. A lot had changed in Iraq, and it seemed that we were moving toward a changing of the guard with the Iraqi forces taking the reigns as we downsized the U.S. presence in the country. We were two months deep, and there was a stand down ordered. There were no U.S. troops leaving the base for about a week.

I had been dealing with the mental strain of the deployment the way I usually did: by staying busy, working out for hours at a time, and sleeping as much as possible when possible. A buddy of mine (you'll meet him later) had a philosophy; if you sleep twelve hours a day, you're only there for six months. After a week of sitting on our duffs, we found out that we were going to be rolling out to the camp where the rest of our unit was located early the next morning. I had trouble sleeping, tossing and turning all night on my cot, as I just could not get myself to relax enough to actually drift off to la la land.

That morning I woke up in a bad mood. It was just one of those days when you're mad at the world from the moment you open your eyes. I had tossed and turned, marinating in my own sweat all night long. Everything felt off. I had a bunch of people I didn't know in my truck. A different soldier was driving for me that day, because

I had given my driver a maintenance day. I guess my platoon sergeant could tell that I was having a rough morning, so he said to me, "Why don't you let LT ride up front today? He needs some practice." I strongly disagreed. I always rode in the front vehicle. Plus, LT had enough on his plate, and there was no way he could realistically try to look for IEDs and command the platoon at the same time. Then I heard the words I'll never forget. My platoon sergeant said, "Don't worry about it. Ain't nothing gonna happen. Just ride today."

The offer did sound appealing. I mean, we had not even found an IED the whole time we'd been there, let alone been hit by one. Other than a couple non-threatening rockets, there was really no trace of enemy contact whatsoever. I complied, thinking to myself that the day would at least be a little less stressful. I was wrong.

I can remember joking around with my driver as we rolled down this desert interstate road with nothing to see. Boxing was a big part of my physical training, and I had delusions of being an amateur boxer, maybe even Golden Gloves. I was telling him how I was going to continue to work hard in the gym while we were there, and when we got back to Texas, I was going to start getting in on some tournaments. In reply, he jokingly told me that boxing was for "brothers and Hispanics," and that I was not the right color to be a good boxer. (Keep in mind, that my driver that day was a black dude. I don't want you picturing some hateful redneck. He was a really squared away troop, too. In the Army, I fought and lived with people of all creeds and colors, and another thing that I am certain of, is that racism is stupid. No race is superior to any other. It's ultimately a sin thing.)

Not gonna lie—what he said hurt my feelings a little. I probably was not going to amount to much because I was a poor boxer who was already moving into his mid-twenties—not because I was white. But then my cockiness and pride took over as I told him, "You see this right hand here?" While shaking my tightly clinched fist in the air, I said, "If I was to hit you with one of these it would be catastrophic." After a short pause and a smirk, I told him, "But gimme six more months, and it would be a cataclysmic, life-altering event if I was to hit you with it." While I was on a roll, I said, "You know what? I might just go ahead and hit you in your shoulder, knock you out that up armored door, and just leave you here on the side of the road. We'll just scoop you up on the way back." **BOOM!**

I had been hit by IED's before, and due to the size of the explosion, I thought we were good. I thought the truck had taken it. Then as the smoke cleared, I realized that my door was gone. The pain in my legs started to set in. I saw the blood gushing from the inside of my left leg. It looked arterial. I had flashbacks of my prior training about how you never wanted to mess up your femoral artery, because it was bad news if you did. My immediate instinct was to put pressure on it. It was then that I noticed that my arm was hanging off. I was not able to move my hand, which is a weird feeling. It was hanging downward towards my elbow as I lifted it up. Right about then was when I flipped out.

Both of my legs were trapped and broken under the collapsed dash of my MRAP armored vehicle. My right hand, that I was so eloquently bragging about just moments earlier, was hanging off with the whole front of my forearm gone. I was covered in fuel, and with smoke everywhere, I wondered if I would burn to death while trapped in that truck. That sounds pretty awful.

Fortunately, I was the worst of the injured. The only other casualty was my gunner who took a piece of shrapnel to his leg. I am also surely blessed to have had a medic in my truck who quickly applied tourniquets to my arm and leg, which were leaking substantially. I am not sure what the situation was with the medevac. Perhaps they could not fly because of a recent dust storm or maybe the quickest option was to do a ground evacuation. That was the option that was chosen by my platoon sergeant. He made the decision that my gunner and I would be loaded into the back of his truck, and regardless of protocol and potential risk, they would get me to medical attention as soon as possible. They were willing to risk their lives to save mine. Jesus said, "Greater love has no one than this: to lay down one's life for one's friends." (John 15:13) The Lieutenant's vehicle would stay back to secure and recover my damaged truck.

Once they finally pried my broken legs out from under my collapsed dash, they carried me on their shoulders like I had just kicked the game winning field goal at the Super Bowl. I am so thankful for the courageous and selfless actions of my platoon on that day—except, for when they threw me into the back of the truck. My foot was hanging out a little bit, and I could not move my leg to get it out of the way. In the chaos and high adrenaline of the situation, one of the younger soldiers kept trying to shut the door and could not figure out why it wouldn't shut. Each time he slammed the door against my foot I would feel the broken pieces of my right femur grind over top of each other. That sucked!

Finally, the issue was resolved, and the truck began to speed towards the closest base with a surgical tent. I was okay at first, but then I started to go into shock. I could no longer move any part of my body. My face seized up. I could not speak. My heart started to beat erratically, and I was having trouble breathing. *Oh no! I think I'm dying,* I thought to myself. Our medic was frantically attempting to get an IV line started on me but was not having any success. I was suddenly hit with the memory of the IED emplacer that I watched die on the side of the road that day during my second tour. I had this dreadful feeling that not only was I going to die, but that I was going to be condemned for the things that I had done. Before the righteous judge of all the earth, I had no case. I was guilty, and I knew it. All I could do was throw myself at the feet of the judge and beg for mercy. So I prayed.

It all happened inside my spirit. There was no audible sound, as I could not speak, but my prayer was clear, and like in the hospital room with my daughter, it was real. I prayed like God was my only hope, because He was. As they were tearing the fuel covered clothes off of me and repeatedly digging in my arm in attempts to find a usable vein, I said this to the Lord Jesus, "I Believe. I believe that you are who you say that you are. I believe that you are the Son of God. I believe that you have the power to forgive my sins. I have lived a horrible life. I have hurt so many people and done so many terrible things. I deserve to die. I deserve to be punished for my sins. But you died for me. Please forgive me, Lord. I am so sorry. Please forgive me. Whether I live or die today, from here on out, I'm yours. Please take care of my girls. I'm ready to go. Amen."

Just as I finished praying, I opened my eyes to see my gunner jump up and snatch the needle out of the medic's hand. Straddling my limp body, bouncing around in the back of a speeding MRAP, with a piece of shrapnel in his own leg, my gunner, Big Baby, stuck me—first try—and got the IV started. It was just saline, salt water basically, but I started to come out of shock. I felt a sense of peace that I had never felt before. It was as if God was holding me in the palm of his hand. I felt as if everything was going to be okay, no matter what happened next. It was the worst thing that ever happened to me, but I have never been more thankful for anything in my life. Whatever road leads to Jesus, no matter how rough, is worth traveling.

When people ask me today about my scars, and I tell them that I got blown up, they usually say something like, "Oh, I'm so sorry." Then I tell them that it was how I met Jesus, and it's the best thing that's ever happened to me.

Chapter 15
No Accidents in the Jesus Game

Now it's time for another story within the story. It was no coincidence that my gunner helped to save my life that day. Oh no! It was clearly planned and divinely orchestrated from above, and there is no convincing me otherwise. If you were wondering why my gunner was able to find a vein when the medic and others had failed, then this might explain it. Big Baby revealed to me that he was an intravenous meth user for several years before joining the Army.

He was not originally part of my squad, but I grew fond of him when I would lead the remedial PT group in my unit for guys that were having trouble meeting weight regulations or passing the PT test. After getting clean, Big Baby put on a ton of weight. I suspect that his thyroid had been damaged or maybe he just did not eat much when he was an addict. Either way, he was having a hard time in the squad he was assigned to and feeling like a redheaded stepchild. It is important for the reader to understand that in the Army there are certain regulations that must be met, and if a soldier does not meet these requirements, then they get "flagged." It's kind of like a military dunce cap.

A soldier who is flagged reflects poorly on their leadership. They cannot be promoted or receive awards. They are kind of like the runt of the litter in some ways. It was clear to me, after spending some time with him, that Big Baby was not enjoying life in his squad. It reminded me of being the fat kid myself as a youngster. It hurt me to see him feeling picked on, left out, and undervalued. He had a good heart, and I felt like I needed to do something. So I went to his squad leader and worked out a trade to bring him over to my team. Some folks questioned my decision, but I knew it was what I needed to do.

I already had a good driver, and you need a good driver over there. (Proud of ya K-Dawg!) You don't want dismounts that are not good on their feet, because they'll slow you down and cause problems on the ground. Plus, the bigger a guy is, the harder he is to drag off the battlefield if he gets hit. The only possible spot was gunner, and he had to be MY gunner, because that's what made it work. It takes a gunner to train a gunner. He made that 50 cal his baby. He was built for it.

Big Baby stood up in the hatch, like I had always done. It's more dangerous, but the gunner can see the road better than anyone in the truck can. I always thought that the front gunner was one of the most important positions in the patrol. Your point man needs to be on his stuff. When you're sitting down at nametape defilade, stuffed down in the hatch like a whack-a-mole at the arcade, you might as well be a passenger in the back of the truck, except for the easy access to a machine gun of course. Even though we were not riding in the front truck that day, Big Baby was still doing his thing, on his feet scanning. He ducked down to get out of the wind so he could light a cigarette right as the IED went off. Big Baby would have been a goner if it had not been for that moment. Interesting.

He was hit with a piece of shrapnel in the leg, which was right next to my head. If Big Baby had not been hit, then he, and his vein striking ability, would not have been in the evacuation vehicle. If I had been hit in the head, it probably wouldn't have mattered anyway. If he had not ducked down to light a smoke, he would have gotten blasted in the face, and the guilt of his death would have been too much for me to bear. If the EFP or shape charge explosive, for the old school vets, went off a little earlier nobody would have been hurt. Life would have continued as usual. If it popped just a little later, then the driver and I would have died and Big Baby would have lost his legs. A little later than that, and I would have lost the four passengers we were carrying in the back of the truck. That would have made for some sleepless nights. Knowing myself, I see that all of these scenarios would have pushed me further away from

God. It happened perfectly in a way that would cause me to lean on God, depending entirely on Him for the salvation of my body and my soul.

All of this timing, and what seemed to be coincidence, is a little bit overwhelming for me. To think that God made it happen in the perfect way to bring about the exact desired result blows my little brain apart. I heard a quote by Kent Hovind one time that really stuck out to me. He said, "The God I worship is not limited by time, space, or matter. If I could fit the infinite God in my three-pound brain He would not be worth worshipping." As I write this, a Bible verse comes to mind from the prophet Isaiah. I'll hit you with the New Living Translation version on this one. "My thoughts are nothing like your thoughts," says the LORD. "And my ways are far beyond anything you could imagine." (Isaiah 55:8 NLT)

God used the one small act of kindness and selfless love, bringing Big Baby into my squad, to save my life months later. If one thing had been off anywhere in the chain of events, then the result would have been completely different. I think God is into math. I am not very good at algebra or any other advanced type of mathematics, but I know this much; if you get one step wrong then it changes the outcome dramatically.

My favorite verse in the entire Bible is Romans 8:28; "And we know that God causes everything to work together for the good of those who love God and are called according to his purpose for them." (NLT) But how is this good? How can God be good and allow suffering? It was the pain that I experienced in the back of that truck that allowed me to really understand the suffering that Jesus experienced on the Cross as He slowly asphyxiated, only able to breath by pushing His weight up on the nails that were driven into His limbs. Now I had experienced a taste of what the Lord had gone through to save me. It was this suffering that made it real for me.

I am convinced that there must come a time when the suffering of Jesus Christ, His sacrifice on that tree, must become personal. He did not have to do that. God could have revealed

Himself to mankind any way that He wanted to. Every single one of the people involved in the crucifixion could have been turned to dust in just a word from the Lord. This guy raised people from the dead, repeatedly. He told storms to shut up and sit down, and they did. In Luke Chapter 4, it says that a synagogue full of angry people mobbed Jesus. They forced him to the edge of a cliff where they were going to push him off. Then it says something interesting; "But he walked right through the crowd and went on his way."

I do not think that this little, often-overlooked story in the Gospels is considered by scholars to be an official miracle, but to me it is probably one of the most impressive things Jesus is reported to have done. I don't know how much experience you have with angry mobs, but I've got a little. When a riot has been incited and people are riled up about something or somebody, you don't just walk through the crowd untouched. You are probably going to need tear gas, rubber bullets, and riot shields. Nope, not Jesus, He just decided that He had backed up far enough. Then He just started walking forward and nobody laid a finger on the one they were enraged at enough to kill.

What people need to realize is that when you can do anything, and I mean anything, then there are no accidents. Jesus did not make a mistake, and the cross served as the consequence. No. Absolutely not! Jesus knew exactly what He was doing. He did it on purpose. The question that faces each of us is, "Why?"

Chapter 16
Keep Your Head Up!

Before we move on in the story, I think it is important to mention that God can use the bad stuff in our lives to bring about good things. My history of childhood bullying led to compassion and empathy for Big Baby. His past drug addiction was used to save my life. It does not mean that we should go on screwing up, treating God like a cosmic janitor running around cleaning up all our messes. But we should be aware that God is willing and able to use our past pain, failure, sins, and heartaches to bring about purpose in our lives if we seek Him. Trust me; God is bigger than you think He is.

"And without faith it is impossible to please God, because anyone who comes to him must believe that he exists and that he rewards those who earnestly seek him." (Hebrews 11:6 NIV)

Unfortunately, I did not know this or trust this right after I got blown up. I knew that something had happened in that truck, in my heart, and if we let our imaginations run wild it is easy to think that once we have felt the presence of God that everything is just smooth sailing after that. This is simply not the case. I think about the Israelites after they had maneuvered through the Red Sea without getting wet. They had been saved. Their enemy was defeated, swimming with the fishes. But as anyone who has been to Sunday School can tell you, the journey was far from over for the Israelites. They had outrun the enemy and been delivered by God's own hand with all of His glorious power, but their tough times and training had only begun.

One might fallaciously think that by some miraculous feat that when I woke up the next day in the green zone hospital, everything was just fine and dandy, happily ever after. That was not the case. Nope, it sucked really bad. I had all of these traumatic

67

injuries that caused my body to hurt constantly. It seemed like I was having another surgery every other day. Some were minor, just to pull out little pieces of shrapnel and clean out wounds. Others were longer and harder to deal with in recovery. The worst part of going into each surgery was knowing that in a few hours I was going to wake up in more pain than I already had. After a few weeks stuck in the bed at Walter Reed Army Medical Center, my spirits had faded.

I was discouraged; I began to hear the voices of doubt and inadequacy as my mind groped around in the fog of a lackluster recovery. I did not know how to deal with what I was going through. Thoughts in the form of statements and questions began to flood my mind continually. It was almost like being shot at, except with negative thoughts instead of bullets. *The Army was the only thing you were ever good at. What are you gonna do now? You can't be a soldier anymore. Am I going to keep my arm? Will my wife still love me? I can't even hold my daughter. What kind of dad am I going to be? They'll be ashamed of you in public; everybody will stare. What if somebody wants to kidnap or rape my family? What can I do? I can't even wipe myself. Look what you're putting them through. Look how sad and angry your wife is; you did that. You've been married for a year and look what she's stuck with. She would be better off without me. She could start over, she and the Boo Boo Bear. She could meet someone that would be able to take care of them, keep them safe, make them happy, somebody that wouldn't be a burden. She's just a baby, she'll never even have to know I ever existed. She won't even remember me.*

It was as if I was teleported back to my dad's bedroom ten years earlier. Everything would be better off if I were dead. It seemed to be the logical conclusion. The worse part was that I could not even come up with a way to do it. I remember actually asking myself the question in my head: "How worthless are you? You can't even kill yourself."

I had been stuck in bed for about three weeks, and my hair looked just ridiculous—think defective Chia Pet. That's a pretty solid comparison. It must have been my first day being successfully transferred into a wheelchair and being able to leave the ward. I was being overwhelmed with suicidal thoughts as GG, my grandmother, pushed me down the long hallway to the barber shop. My head was hanging low as I stared at the passing tiles on the floor of the long fluorescent-lit hallway. It was without a doubt, the lowest valley I had ever been in. Just then I heard a voice, "Keep your head up." Half wondering if he was talking to me or someone else; my eyes rose to behold a sight they had never seen before.

It was a kid who could not have been old enough to drink. If he was, you would still card him every time. He had lost all four limbs and an eye. A stump of a human being sitting up on a hospital bed being rolled down the hall in the direction opposite me. In my mental funk I did not even notice him until he spoke to me. We made eye contact, and he said, "Keep your head up. It gets better." It blew me away. This kid had lost everything, and even in the midst of his suffering, he took the time to make the deliberate effort to cheer me up. That was it; the spark I needed to shift my focus and tell the voices in my head to shut up. I decided in that moment that I would not put my head down anymore. If this guy could stay motivated, and be an encouragement to others, then I had no excuse.

The truth is, God used that young man to save my life. He was at the right place at the right time and in the right condition. If anyone else would have told me to keep my head up, it would have gone in one ear and out the other. But because of the source, the statement had a lot of weight to it. God used that young man as a pivotal transition point in my life. What he said stuck with me only because of the suffering he had experienced.

If I had any doubts—which I didn't—that God placed that young man directly in my path that day, then what I would later learn about him would have changed all that. For the sake of your own doubts, I will let you know some more interesting "coincidental" facts. It turns out that at almost the same moment that I was experiencing God, really, for the first time, Easter Sunday in 2009, when the Lord spared the life of my precious Boo Boo Bear, that fine young man was getting blown up. Then in turn, he was at the exact right place at the perfect time to say ten words to me in the form of two short sentences that would completely change my life. It was the only time I ever saw him. The only time I ever spoke to him, and I didn't even say a word.

I went to his Facebook page one time to leave him a message; saying thank you for being a saving light in my darkest hours. He never wrote me back, but I came across an interview that he did in one of the mainstream news stories that covered his miraculous recovery from the brink of what should have been certain death. In that story, this fine young hero expressed that, even though it was very tough to deal with everything he had been through, he still trusted that it was part of a plan, the plan of a good God. I agree. Once again, God had used a person, and the results of something evil, to spring forth something good. "The light shines in the darkness, and the darkness has not overcome it." (John 1:5 NIV)

Chapter 17
All In

In the Army we played cards a lot. Most folks think about the action-packed and arduous moments of combat. There are those for certain, but there are far more dead spaces where you just have to pass the time without becoming homesick or perishing from extreme boredom. It turns out, that being stuck in a place that you don't want to be, with nothing to do, really stinks. So, you play cards.

Spades was always my favorite. I even have a tattoo of a big Joker because of the affinity my platoon had for the game during my second deployment. During this deployment in Northern Iraq was also when I was first introduced to the game of Texas Holdem. It is the type of poker that they play on TV. Growing up, I played Five Card Draw, but I never played Holdem until that second deployment. I fell in love almost immediately. Each person only has two cards, and everything else is face-up on the table. There are a lot of head games involved.

We used to have a weekly poker tournament in our platoon. Each player would toss in twenty bucks, and at the end of it, third place would get their money back, second would double up, and first place gets the rest. I used to always play pretty conservatively, hoping to always stick it out to the end and at least get my money back. I found that I was pretty effective at this tactic, but I was not winning any money. Eventually, I would just get nickel and dimed to death as the blinds grew higher, until I did not really have enough chips to make a difference.

I learned that there was a certain point in the game when you're going to have to put your chips in based on the strength of your hand and the position in which you find yourself. At some point, if you want to win, you have to go ALL IN. But it is the hardest decision that you face throughout the entire game, because

71

of what is at stake. If it works out, then you double your chips, possibly more, and set yourself up to make a run at the first place cash—or, you lose everything and watch the rest of the tournament from the sidelines.

I think that we can live our lives the same way. We are afraid that if we put it all out there and fully dedicate ourselves to a God who many others do not believe in, we may lose; it may cost us everything. But if we remain lukewarm and half-hearted, then it gives us room to back away if the cards turn and the odds look bad. We reserve the opportunity to fold. Another issue with going "all in" is that question lurking in the back of your head: "What if there is something better?" So you sit there thinking you got the best hand, but you're not one-hundred percent sure. Then a player you're up against forces you to make a decision. The bet on the table is more than you have to offer. You go all in, or you fold, give them some of your chips, but get to keep enough to limp down the road a little longer. At the end of the day, you still lose.

There came a point in time when I decided that I was going to put all my chips in on Jesus. I was persuaded that God is real, that Jesus is His Son, that He died to forgive and save me, and that He had spared my life for a reason. I also realized that I did not really know this God.

There was a chaplain at Walter Reed who came into my room one day. I did not really like the other chaplain that had been assigned to me, but I was refreshed by this chaplain's visit. I do not remember the visit well, I guess because of the pain meds, but I do remember him giving me a green leather army-edition Bible. It had my rank and name etched into it with gold lettering. I thought it was really cool, but I had never really done any Bible reading. When I did, it was the King James Version, and I never really got much out of it.

I decided that I was going to really get to know this God, whom I claimed to believe in. I like to tell folks that I knew Jesus like I know Michael Jordan. I can tell you stats, how many championships he won, where he went to school, but I don't really know Michael Jordan. The same could be said of Jesus and the Bible in general. I knew Sunday School stories. I knew the reason for the season at Christmas time and why lots of people went to church on Easter Sunday. But I did not really know Jesus. Having determined that there is a God, and that Jesus is as close as you are ever going to get to God, I decided that I was going to learn everything I could about Him.

Church became a regular part of our life, as my wife and I would attend the service at the chapel on the campus at Walter Reed. Once I was discharged from inpatient care, we lived in a hotel with a bunch of other wounded troops, and I had a pretty sweet motorized wheelchair. I had plenty of time on my hands, and Bible reading became more frequent.

The months we spent living at the Malone House at Walter Reed were tough, but we were certainly blessed. I could feel myself healing physically, mentally, and spiritually. There was also another person during this time period who helped me immensely. I called her the "feelings whisperer." She was the psychologist I saw regularly for several months while recovering from my injuries. She helped me to realize so many things about who I was and how I saw the world around me. Somehow, she managed to get the feelings—good, bad, and ugly—to come rolling out of me—hence the nickname. These intense therapy sessions showed me who I was, and the Word of God showed me where I needed to change.

It was a challenging and often stressful period of time for me and for our marriage, but after a few months, I was on my feet again, and we were headed back to Fort Bliss to begin the next chapter in good ole El Paso Texas. I was starting to learn that when you decide to go all in with God, He makes sure you get dealt the right cards.

Chapter 18
The Man Who Didn't Wear Shorts

After I was transferred from Walter Reed back to Fort Bliss, I began to yearn and hunger for the things of God like never before in my life. I dug into the Gospels, often reading them straight through in a day. Jesus began to absolutely fascinate me. Every time I would read a Gospel account, there would be new things that would jump off the page and speak to my heart. I could feel myself changing.

Hebrews 4:12 says, "For the Word of God is alive and active. Sharper than any double-edged sword, it penetrates even to dividing soul and spirit, joints and marrow; it judges the thoughts and attitudes of the heart." (NIV) I began to experience this for the very first time as I spent hours reading. God's Word is also compared to bread and to living water many times throughout scripture. To be honest, I am blessed to say that I really have no idea what it is like to starve or suffer from real prolonged hunger. I have missed a few meals here and there, but never for any meaningful period of time. That being said, having spent a lot of time in gyms and deserts, I do know what it's like to thirst.

God's Word is also described as living water. Spiritually, I felt as if I had been out running through the desert and finally found cold, clear, smooth water. Because of my injuries, I was in a Warrior Transition Unit. This is a place where you sit on your butt until the Army decides what it wants to do with you. I sat and read the Bible for hours, falling deeper and deeper in love with the God I found in the person of Jesus Christ. I could not get enough of this water. James 4:8 says, "Draw near to God, and He will come near to you." I found this to be quite true. I was praying more and more, and I would see the prayers answered.

Spiritually, I was growing like Kudzu, but I still found myself in a fight with the old me. There were things that I was reading that I did not understand. I was scared to go to church, even though I knew it was where I should be. I was practicing my faith mostly in private, because even though I knew I was saved, I still felt like the worst person in the room when I went to church. How could I ever serve God? How could I tell someone else about God after everything I'd done?

I have heard it said by several preachers that, "every Paul needs a Timothy, and every Timothy needs a Paul." I think it works this way for women too, but I know it's true for guys. We need some people around that help us to grow, hold us accountable, and teach us the things we do not yet know, or perhaps what we have forgotten. What I'm talking about is mentorship. These relationships are pivotal for our spiritual development. I think that in order to really live out the Christian life, we should be serving as a mentor and a mentee constantly, always led and always leading.

During this time of transition for my family and me, my mind was often troubled with trying to figure out who I was going to be, and what I was going to do, once the Army said that my services were no longer required. I knew that God had spared my life, but I had no idea why. Then God placed another person in my path that would greatly contribute to my spiritual growth.

As a family, we had started periodically attending a church right down the street from our house. I still didn't feel comfortable. We soon faded in our attendance. Then one night a tall, kind of lanky guy with glasses showed up at my door. After having seen what people are capable of, I am understandably guarded and skeptical of strangers who show up at my door unannounced.

I think he caught me on a bad day. I was in a bad mood, in the middle of an argument, or something of that sort, when I heard the knock on the door. I remember being a little standoffish towards him, thinking that he was probably some type of salesman, there to inconvenience my evening. He told me that he was there to give us a flyer and invite us to the church where he attended about a half a mile down the road. It was a brief discussion, cordial, but short-lived. He went on his way, and I took the flyer and tossed it on a table, thinking little about it.

I am not sure how long it was afterwards, but one Sunday, we decided that we would give that church a shot. When we got there the first Sunday, I felt that feeling you have when you are going into a place full of complete strangers, and you immediately start looking for people you know. I hate that feeling. I didn't find anybody. My wife, the baby, and I made our way into the very back of the balcony in the large church sanctuary. It was almost like we expected it to probably be the first and last time we would ever be there, so there was no point interacting with anybody or even being seen by them. I also despised feeling judged by strangers as they stare at "the new people."

As the service was about to start, I finally spotted a familiar face. It was the guy who had come to my door that night. He was seated on the stage at the front of the assembly. It turned out that the lanky guy with glasses was an associate pastor at the church. The service was nice but felt more like going to the movies than church. There were so many people there that all I could think about was escaping as quickly as possible once it was over.

Completely to my surprise, that associate pastor showed up at my door again a couple of nights later. I thought we had stayed off the radar, but apparently, he had spotted us at the church service. I guess the reason that I hate thinking about people judging me is because of my own judgmental and stereotypical thoughts that I have toward folks. In other words, if they are thinking about me the same way I'm thinking about them, then that ain't good. My first thought was that this guy was going to be some kind of song singing cheerleader, too weird to be seen with in public, or, he would be a tasteless, miserable, Bible thumper, running around trying to make people as miserable as himself. I'm just being honest.

But this man of God was neither of those things. In fact, he was actually pretty cool. He was from West Virginia, an athlete like me. A man's man, as some would say. We talked sports teams and even engaged in a little friendly ball busting. It really meant a lot to me that he remembered where I lived, and that it was important to him that I was aware that he saw me at church the prior Sunday. Then, to my complete astonishment, the pastor invited my wife and me to lunch at his house with his family after the service on the following Sunday. I have heard a lot of folks use this quote that I suppose could be attributed to Teddy Roosevelt; "Nobody cares how much you know until they know how much you care." It really is true.

Over the next couple of years, my family and I attended services regularly at that church. We even went to some Sunday School classes from time to time. It was a difficult time for me, the space between getting blown up and getting medically retired from the Army. I felt like Abraham, when God told him, "Go from your country, your people, and your father's household to the land I will show you." (Genesis, 12:1) It was mostly unanswered questions that got to me the most. I knew that I was alive for a reason. I just had no idea what the reason was. Then there was also the battle, which remains constant, old me vs. new me. I had too much time on my hands, and very little to do as I was just sitting around waiting to see what the Army was going to do with me.

At the Warrior Transition Unit, the higher ups decided that everyone who was able, needed to start doing some type of work in alignment with what they planned to do after being separated from the military. I started taking some college courses online and figured that maybe I would be a teacher and a football coach. Then, they came back and said that part-time college courses did not count. Apparently, they wanted several hours of actual documented work per week. I was still pretty banged up, more than most of the troops there, and I could have probably whined my way out of it, but I used it as an opportunity to get closer to God.

I went to visit the pastor one day, and I asked if I could come down and pitch in around the church a few days a week. When I explained the situation to him, he gladly obliged my volunteer request. I showed up after lunch and worked there doing odds and ends until close of business formation at 1700. It was mainly just busy work, and to be honest, it was probably an inconvenience to the pastor to find any work for me to do at all. But he did and did it with a great attitude that always made me feel welcome.

The days at the church would always start the same. I would pull into the parking lot in my 1996 Chevy SS Impala on twenty-two-inch rims, bumping some type of obnoxious southern rap through a couple of massive subwoofers. I would walk in the side door and down to the pastor's office. Sometimes he was in there, sometimes not. I would go in and sit down regardless. I really looked forward to this part. The pastor and I would usually get to spend about thirty minutes talking each day. It was in these times that I could ask the questions that would be running through my head as I studied my Bible, the things I struggled with mentally and emotionally, my past sins and my current ones.

The pastor always had an answer, good answers, and if he did not have it, he was going to get it. One of his answers really stuck with me and has changed the way that I view religion. One day I was sweeping the basketball court as the pastor came in from some outside sports activity. It was summertime in El Paso, so it was ridiculously hot. I noticed that the pastor was wearing pants, and I commented on it saying, "It's too dang hot to be wearing pants. We need to get you some shorts, man." He simply replied, "I don't wear shorts." It blew my mind. "What?! It's 105 degrees outside. Are you serious?"

He explained that it was something that God convicted him about, and, as a man of God, he wants to honor the Lord in every way. I asked him if the Bible said it was wrong to wear shorts, and I kind of sarcastically asked if I should stop wearing shorts too, pointing to the pair I was wearing at the time. It was in this conversation that I learned the difference between religion and relationship. The pastor loved Jesus so much that he was wearing pants in the 105-degree desert heat, even though he didn't theologically have to. It was just something he did, or didn't do, for the Lord. Religion says that you must adhere to this list of demands performed at the behest of a distant god who is excited to smite those who disobey. Relationship is living a life of devotion, submission, and gratitude for God's amazing grace and unending love. God is a person, and His fullest revelation is found in Jesus, and until religion turns into relationship, there will always be insurmountable distance between God and us. The Bible didn't condemn shorts, it was just something between a man and his God.

Chapter 19
The Mount of Transfiguration

There are an abundance of passages in scripture that reference spending time with God on the mountain. We see it in Exodus as Moses would go up into the cloud on Mount Sinai for forty days at a time. One time the Israelite's leader came down off the mountain, and he was glowing so brightly that it freaked out everybody that saw him. It was on the mountain where Moses received the Commandments from The Lord. There are also many references to Jesus pulling out from the hustle and bustle of endless activity that accompanied His teaching and healing ministry. If Jesus, the eternal Son of God, needed to spend time alone with His Father while here in human form, then how much more do we need it?

When the Army medically retired me in 2012, we went back to my hometown in Carolina. After praying considerably and thinking a lot about what we desired in a home, we came across a beautiful house near a lake on top of a mountain. It was on this mountain where my relationship with God was formed, where a friendship was made.

The loss of identity that I felt, no longer being in the Army, heightened my desire to find out who I am and what my purpose is. In Paul's second letter to the Corinthians he writes, "Therefore, if anyone is in Christ, the new creation has come: The old has gone, the new is here!" (5:17 NIV) What does that mean? If I am not who I always have been, then who am I?

A.W. Tozer wrote, "What comes to our mind when we think about God is the most important thing about us." I think that this is one of the most brilliantly simple expressions of truth that I have ever heard. When I think about God, I think of a Sovereign Ruler who created galaxies with the words of His mouth. But not just that, He is intimately involved and deeply loves creation. His love for people is so strong that He entered into their desperate and fallen state, to live among them as God and man simultaneously.

When I think about God, I think of Jesus—the real deal Jesus. I look at His life, and I can learn what God is like. God is not only all of the things that I mentioned before, but also a person. God knows us better than we know ourselves and still loves us more than we could ever comprehend. There are no accidents with God. What we see in the life of Jesus is exactly what God intends for us to see. There comes a time for each of us when that must become personal.

Everything that Jesus did was intentional. His life clearly displays that He could heal the sick, blind, lame, deaf, leprous, paralyzed, crazy, bleeding, and possessed. Jesus also had control over life and death, displayed in His raising several people from the dead, and Himself. Oh yeah, Jesus also controlled the weather from time to time, walked on water, teleported a boat, and did some pretty sweet tricks with food and wine. So, why did He allow Himself to be beaten? Why not just power-up and blast the Sanhedrin into oblivion? Then they would have believed! Why not make the Cross float? Why try to carry it up the hill? It's the question that slaps everyone in the face if they think too long about it. Why did Jesus allow Himself to be crucified and die?

If God just wanted us to believe in Him, then He could have done that easily a million other ways. He could have revealed Himself as a 300-foot-tall flying giant. But God wanted us to know Him and how much He deeply cares for us. He is our Father. I could not understand the love of God until I had children. As I held them in my arms for the first time, experiencing that feeling, I realized that's the way that God feels about me. That's the way God feels about you.

Once I truly let it sink in, that even though I was a sack of hot garbage in my own eyes, God loved me and had a purpose for my life. It filled me with gratitude and a desire to seek Him even more diligently. It seemed that the more I sought God, the more opportunities to find God would present themselves. I acknowledged that I had no idea what my ultimate purpose was, but I knew it would be in service to God in some way, shape, or form.

I changed my major from secondary education to Christian studies with an emphasis on youth ministry. Instead of just reading the Bible recreationally, I started to really study it, seeing God's word in new ways that I never noticed or thought about before. I was finding the answers to all of the questions and doubts that clouded my heart and mind. Books written about the Bible and the Patriarchs of Early Christianity began to reinforce my philosophy about the beauty of relationship and the dangers of religiosity. But I also found myself struggling with the plight of my fellow man. I had been seeking God fairly diligently for a few years at this point and felt as if I was just beginning to scratch the surface. I had reached a point at which I was finally secure in my own salvation, a point at which I had a growing dynamic relationship with Christ; love had transformed my inner being, and light had cast out a great deal of the darkness within my soul. But what about those who are not seeking?

A lot had changed since my days of drinking, fighting, and acting a fool, but nevertheless, I found myself at a party. It was not the type of place where you would find a "Christian." There was drinking and other questionable behaviors happening. But, all in all, everybody there seemed like generally good people. A realization hit me pretty early in the evening. I was the only one present who had a relationship with Christ. There was the occasional insult thrown towards people of faith referring to "Bible thumpers" and "church folks" in a way that made believers seem to be inferior. There was animosity in their voices, and I could clearly see that at some point in time something had happened that caused resentment towards the God of the Christian faith, the Bible, and the church. This resentment mixed with the doubts, questions, conflicting belief systems, opinions, and just the general state of living in a fallen and broken world had plunged every other person at that party into a state of apathetic agnosticism. They did not know if there was a god or not, and they did not really seem to care.

It was at this party that I had a vision. I suppose that is what it would be called. It was not a dream, because I was very much awake, and I do not really know what to compare it to because it was really the only time it has ever happened to me. I have had some pretty vivid flashbacks to stuff that happened in Iraq, but this was different.

There were about eight of us sitting in the living room, gathered around a large coffee table, some on the floor, some seated on the furniture, talking and listening to music, when, out of nowhere, it was as if a blast went off. The only thing that I can think of that I had ever seen that was similar is the internet video of an atomic blast. All of the people in the room were instantly swept from right to left, like the turning of a page. But around me was a bubble or some type of force field, which left me completely unaffected by the blast wave that had swept the others through the wall on the left side of the room. Inside my bubble was peace, harmony, and a still, muffled, almost silent hum. It was very similar to being in a recording studio with the headphones on right before the music starts. Those moments when you become aware of your own breathing and can feel and hear your heart beating in your ears.

Then, just as suddenly as it had come, the vision disappeared. I crashed back into reality and was pleasantly surprised that no one even realized I had briefly departed. I immediately got up and made my way to the door attempting to get outside in search of some much-needed fresh air. I was physically shaken by the event, and troubled deep in my soul. I decided that it would be best if I slept there, instead of trying to drive over an hour back to the house late at night. Tossing and turning back and forth, unable to find rest, I watched the slits of the window on the east side of the house until the first rays of morning sun started poking through.

I can remember this distinct desire to be alone with God, to start figuring out what I had experienced the night before. By this point, I realized that God's Spirit often communicates through God's Word. As I prayed on the drive home, continually asking God what this vision meant, something that I had read in Matthew's Gospel immediately came into my thoughts. It was the explanation that Jesus gave to His parable about the wheat and the weeds. In this explanation, Jesus say's that He will send His angels to reap the harvest on earth. First, the angels will go and collect all of the weeds from the field. This is all of the evildoers and everything that causes sin. These weeds are to be bundled up and thrown into the fire. Then subsequently, the wheat, which is the righteous, godly, and good in the world, will be harvested into Heaven.

Then came the light bulb moment—a spiritual epiphany of sorts. It was something that I did not want to ever really think about, but now it was staring me in the face. A lot of people are on their way to hell and they're completely unaware of it. Because they want nothing to do with God in this life, they would be eternally separated from Him and all things good. Forever. As long as you can think of, time multiplied by infinity in a place of darkness, weeping, and gnashing of teeth. This is the way that Jesus described this place. As I was on the last stretch of road before reaching my house that morning, my mind began to painfully ponder each of these things.

Darkness has always scared me, and it still does. Even after three tours in Iraq, I am still afraid of the dark. I prefer a sunrise to a sunset any day of the week. I am also well aware of what it is that causes a man to weep. Deep loss, disappointment, broken heartedness, when your emotions are too much for you to bear, that feeling that causes you to consider ending your own life. These are the sources of weeping. I have wept many times in this short existence on earth, but there are only a few times I have gnashed my teeth. The one time that really sticks out in my mind is when they got me into the back of the evac vehicle when I got blown up. As I said before, my right femur was broken clean right above the knee. Well, they did not get my tall body back far enough into the truck, and my foot was still partially hanging out of the door. One of the

84

soldiers, clearly rattled by the current events, kept trying to shut the up-armored door of the MRAP but could not seem to figure out why it would not shut. Each time he would slam that door the broken pieces of my bone would grind against each other. This is gnashing of teeth.

Tears filled my eyes as I thought about the future awaiting so many souls, and an incredible burden to reach the lost was placed on my heart. I began to cry so hard that I had to pull the truck over to the side of the road. I wept in this moment, not for myself, but for others who were lost and yet had no idea.

The other day, I experienced this concept of being lost yet completely unaware of it. I plugged a well-known historical landmark into the GPS on my phone where I was going to a speaking engagement. I was sure that the map was leading me in the right direction and that I would soon arrive exactly at my destination. The only problem: my map was wrong. It said that I had arrived, but I looked around and there was nothing in sight. My heart began to race, and panic set in, as I realized that I had somewhere to be but no idea how to get there. I thought I had it all figured out until I realized that I did not have a clue.

What do you want me to do Lord? I am ready to serve you. The thought of how destroyed God must be, that He had sent His Son into the world to die for us, yet we are content to live a life apart from Him, wallowing in our own filth. It must absolutely tear Him up to see it. Before, I had sought God for my own salvation, forgiveness, peace of heart and mind, blessings for my family and friends, but now my sole objective was to find out what God wanted me to do. I had been transformed from lost to found, and now it was time for me to become God's hand in the life of others.

Part 2

The Epic Adventures
of Team Jesus

Chapter 1
Go Forth!

There are some things in life that are passing fads, momentary affections that are here today and gone tomorrow. For example, the bowl cut or JNCO jeans, in my particular case. These momentary infatuations are, in my opinion, due to our fallen state of depravity. But there are also those things that are coded into our DNA by our Creator that orient us toward and enable us to accomplish the divine purpose for our lives in this temporary existence on planet earth. There are also the many other influential factors in the mosaic that is our lives. In short, I believe that we are undoubtedly a result of nature and nurture. But I also affirm that neither of these things are outside the influence and sovereign majesty of the All-powerful God. In fact, I think that when we seek God diligently, He will work all of these factors into our greater purpose of bringing glory to His Kingdom.

All of these things came together for me in 2014. Having met Jesus, having looked death in the face, I wanted to serve Him. What could I do? I knew God had a mission for me, and every time I was alone, the weight of it would rest upon my soul, feeling as if an elephant were sitting on my chest. It was all I could think about—lost souls, suffering people, who were missing out on the greatest thing that they could possibly imagine. A world full of people was deciding to have little or nothing to do with its Creator and destined for an eternity without Him. It was all that I could see everywhere I went. I heard a sermon from Billy Graham that spoke about the indecisiveness of man. As everyone who is familiar with the late evangelist can tell you, Billy's entire objective was to bring you to a decision. On the fence was not an option. He equated it to catching a flight at the airport. For instance, if you stand around at the terminal long enough trying to make up your mind, then eventually that plane will leave and the choice will have been made for you. If we fail to make a decision long enough, then the decision will inevitably be made for us.

I decided that I was all-in with Jesus and that I was going to go headfirst into whatever He was putting on my heart. It became the focal point of each of my prayers. It became the focal point of my entire life. I went to my wife one night and said to her, "I think Jesus wants me to do something big and maybe even kinda crazy." She was caught off guard by my approach, but nevertheless, she replied that she would support me regardless of the situation. My concern was that I may be put into a position where I may have to choose between my wife and my God, in which case, I would have to side with the Lord. I certainly did not want to ever have to choose. It meant a lot to me that she had my back, even though neither of us really had any idea what was around the bend, only that it was going to be a game changer.

At first, I envisioned this astonishing series of Billy Graham style evangelistic crusades and Christian celebrations that would bring the body of Christ together in a way that no one had ever seen before. I suppose it was just because that was the only real exciting and motivating style of evangelism I had ever seen. I certainly believed that God could make it happen, but I suppose it was a bit ambitious and naive to think that a wounded veteran with no ministry experience and only a small amount of formal theological education would be able to orchestrate the largest revival in the history of our nation. I went for it anyway. I did not want to limit God's ability to work in my life and to manifest His will because I had little faith. I can remember a story in the Gospels where Jesus was limited in His miracle working power because of a lack of faith in the people of that region.

I had this vision of leading a convoy of hundreds of cars all over the country, having rallies in every state in the continental US. The original goal was forty-eight states in forty-eight days—one million souls for Jesus. Yeah, pretty ambitious right? I knew I was going to need a lot of help and coordination to turn this idea into a reality. This resulted in me emailing and calling hundreds of churches and pastors all over the country. Almost nothing came of these contacts, in fact, what feedback I did receive was mainly just discouraging.

Negative thoughts started to creep into my mind. Was I delusional? Had I somehow made it all up inside my Post Traumatic Stress Disorder (PTSD) riddled brain? Was this just my own way of attempting to counter the lack of purpose that I now felt as a result of leaving the military? Perhaps, like the ridiculous bowl cut I had in sixth grade, this was just a passing affinity that would be better off left behind.

I was discouraged, disappointed, and frankly, quite confused about the whole thing. I knew God had called me to do this, but everything was against me, and there appeared to be no change in sight. The plan was to get everything planned and coordinated so that we would be able to take off June 15, 2015. It was already March and nothing had come together. There was no coordination or communication with churches in the planned destinations, only a few hundred dollars saved, and all of the observable facts pointed towards either a non-starter or a catastrophic defeat and failure to complete. But even in the midst of all this external evidence to the contrary, I still could hear that Still Small Voice of the Holy Spirit urging me onward. Whenever I would open God's Word, I would clearly feel the unmistakable call to go.

It reminded me of the feeling when you are in the gunner's hatch of the Humvee and you are not really sure whether you see an IED or not. There comes a time when you got to make a choice. Either we are going to call out the Explosive Ordinance Disposal Unit (EOD) and wait for four hours while they dig around with a robot and finally do a controlled detonation. Or, they come to you with the disappointing news that there really was no IED, and you just wasted four hours of everybody's life and probably caused them to miss chow. The other choice was to hunker down, stomp on the gas pedal, and hope for the best. I suppose I have always been partial to option two.

Even though very influential people in my life were advising me that I should abort the whole thing, my mind was again and again brought to the great commission found at the end of Matthew's Gospel. Jesus says to His disciples, "All authority in Heaven and on earth has been given to me." Let that soak in for a second. All authority, not some, not a lot, all, every bit of it belongs to Him. The very next thing He says is, "Go Forth and make disciples of all nations." No matter how bad things looked, I could not get this commission out of my head. So, one night, in tears on my knees, I cried out to the Lord, and said, "I'm all in no matter what." I will go. If it breaks me, so be it. If it kills me, what better way to go? If I lose everything and fail, at least I can say I stepped out of the boat and tried to walk on the water. That's when things started to pop.

Chapter 2
The Dude

My platoon during the second tour in Iraq was a close-knit family. Our nickname was the Hoodang clan. I have come to find out that in virtually every organization there is someone who keeps everyone connected. It is usually someone who runs their mouth a lot. For us that person is Rex. I kind of think of him as the operator, as he never fails to give us a call to check in on the old crew from time to time, just to make sure that we are still kicking.

One night, Rex called me up to tell me that The Dude was not doing well. I first met The Dude during my first deployment in the sandbox. We were in the same battalion, but a different company. We were in the middle of a battalion fun day when we got the call. The message that I received was that a car bomb had gone off on a platoon in Bravo Battery. Our platoon was on QRF (quick reaction force) that day, so it was our responsibility to get there as quickly as possible to render aid and recover the vehicle or whatever was left of it. I recall somebody saying something like "bring body bags."

As we rolled into a pretty rough part of the city not very far from our base, I did not know quite what to expect. We had been in country for a good while at this point, so we had seen many things, and our cherries were all fully popped. Most of my time was spent in the gunner's hatch, so I got the privilege of getting to look at things that those in the truck missed. I was the gunner at the front of the convoy on that day, and I saw something I had not seen before. As we pulled up to the scene, I realized that I was able to see through the windshield of the damaged Humvee, from the back! The entire back of the truck was just gone. The taxicab that detonated, packed full of artillery rounds, had completely disappeared.

I don't know if I prayed or not, but I was genuinely afraid of what I was going to see next. There was no doubt in my mind that

91

multiple severe casualties would be the next things that my eyes would see. I had already witnessed death, caused by myself and others, but I constantly feared that one day I would come face to face with a dead, young, American boy like me. It's almost not real until it happens to somebody you really know and have spent time with, so you can kind of keep your head above water by pretending it can't come close to you.

Our platoon sergeant told the driver to pull right up beside the excessively disabled vehicle. I was looking inside the truck from my gunner's hatch to see if there were any bodies or body parts inside. Our platoon sergeant jumped out and started looking for the injured personnel. I see someone from Bravo point over to the curb off to the right side, and there sat three soldiers, all in one piece, except for looking like they wound up on the wrong end of a bar fight. It was the crew of the blown-up vehicle: driver, gunner, and Truck Commander. The dismount that usually sat in the backseat apparently had just gone on R&R. How about that? I was amazed. I'm still amazed. I think it was a miracle. Divine intervention. The gunner of that vehicle was The Dude.

The Dude would end up in the same platoon as me for the next tour in Iraq, Hoodang! We were very different, he and I, but I always admired his intelligence and MacGyverish ability to accomplish almost anything. After receiving the orders from Rex to check on The Dude, I walked outside so that I could give him a call. We made a little small talk at first, and then I asked him what was going on. His older brother had died tragically and unexpectedly, and The Dude was the first to find him. It broke my heart to hear it, and I could only imagine the agony that he was going through. At this time, I still struggled with my demons, the thoughts and emotional damage from combat experiences. I still do. But I could only imagine the battle that he must be experiencing. Jesus had helped me immensely with everything that I dealt with, and my mind was being made new all the time.

So, I figured I would share what God had done for me, and that He could help The Dude with what he was dealing with. But he shut me down pretty quickly. He said something to the effect of, "I'm glad that you got right with God, and I'm glad it helped you get through everything, but I really don't wanna hear it right now." It was not said angrily or disrespectfully. It was said in a very loving and hurting tone. He really was genuinely happy that I had found a source of peace, but I could tell that God and The Dude had some issues to work out and were not necessarily on speaking terms at the moment. I told The Dude that I loved him. I started praying for him.

I will not go into details because he has his own story to tell, but The Dude went through a tough time after that. He wrestled with God. By checking him out on Facebook every now and then and seeing some of things he would post, I could tell that he was in a dark place. So every time The Dude crossed my mind, I prayed for him. There are times when you feel like your prayers are having the opposite effect that you hoped for. This was one of those times, but that is why it is so important to have faith and to believe that no matter what the score is, we are still going to win the game.

I did not call or try to share the Gospel with him; he knew the Gospel. I did not send him text messages with Bible verses in them. I prayed for him, regularly. I trusted that God was going to find some way to reveal Himself, to bring peace to the battlefield of the soul. Then, in March 2015, I got a voicemail from The Dude. I'm not sure why I missed the call, but I was blown away when I heard what he said. Apparently, in the middle of the night he had a spiritual experience and decided to recommit his life to Jesus Christ. The war between The Dude and God was over, and he had transferred from an enemy to a child of God.

It was like getting struck with lightning on a sunny day. It could not have caught me more off guard. I was standing in a convenience store, and I remember making quite a scene. I called him back right away, but he was asleep. So I left him a voice mail, and anxiously awaited his call for the next few hours. I cannot remember being more excited. It was like Christmas morning. Even greater joy came in our conversation later that day, as The Dude asked me if he could join me on the mission trip that I was going on that summer. He said that he would drive out to Carolina from all the way in New Mexico to help me prepare, organize, and execute this massive undertaking from God to reach the lost and love the hurting.

It turns out that not only did God answer my prayers for The Dude, but also for myself. This was the boost I needed. I had a partner I could trust, who could split the driving time with me and double our effectiveness and efficiency. Plus, he had numerous different skills dealing with mechanics and carpentry that I simply did not have, and the tools to go with them. There is no such thing as a perfect partnership, because there are no perfect people, but this was pretty darn close.

Then speaking opportunities at local churches started popping up, basically out of nowhere. I was given the humbling honor of being able to go to local churches of many denominations to share my testimony and collect an offering for the purpose of visiting all forty-eight states of the continental U.S. and affecting as many lives as possible in forty-eight days. We also received donations of Gospel tracts and Bibles. It was amazing how quickly and randomly everything came together. After I had been working so hard for almost a year, with absolutely no real success. In the span of two months, it all just fell into place. God working through His people did it all. The things I did amounted to crumbs, but the things God did made it all come together—not in my strength, but His. That's why He gets the glory and not me.

I do not think I could have done it without The Dude. He was absolutely instrumental in getting the mission off the ground and stayed in the fight from beginning to end to make sure that it was executed to success. I cannot thank him enough for helping my vision to serve the Lord become a reality.

Chapter 3
Living in a Van

As the final days counted down before our departure, I could not fight the familiar feeling that I was deploying into combat again. The funds were raised, supplies purchased, bags packed, and arrangements made. It was happening. The time to turn back had passed, and all there was to do was to kiss the wife and kids and see what the future holds. Though we had put a great deal of planning in, there were so many variables that no one could forecast. These unknowns cause a subtle anxiety that keeps you from really being present and soaking in those last few hours with the ones you love. There is a lingering feeling that if you hug them too long you won't ever actually leave.

We rented a U-Haul cargo van, customized it to where we would be able to carry everything we needed and still have a place to sleep at night. It was perfect for a couple of combat vets, who had slept in some pretty tight and uncomfortable circumstances. Nice and cozy. Fortunately, we did not have to sleep in it every night. There were people through our connections with family, church, and the Army who would take us in for a night so that we could get a shower and sleep in a nice comfy bed. I cannot thank them enough either. They have no idea how much those brief respites of comfort between days in the streets meant to us. It was so kind of them to provide for us and take in a couple of sweaty, smelly, rough-around-the-edges vets who had been hanging out with homeless people all day.

Originally, we had only planned on distributing Bibles and Gospel tracts, praying with people, and sharing the Gospel and personal testimony when the opportunity presented itself. Our first stop was in Columbia, South Carolina. It was 102 degrees. We spent a couple of hours walking around downtown where the most people seemed to be congregating. Several people accepted the things we were offering, but when we would come across the homeless and impoverished, they needed water, one thing that we did not bring enough of. We also noticed that when we would give someone a cold bottle of water, it would open up an opportunity for conversation and prayer. We constantly needed cold water ourselves and would always have some on us in the extremely hot streets, so we decided early on that cold water would be part of our daily ministry.

When we got to Savannah, Georgia on day two, we came across significantly more homeless people than the day before, and we began to understand that they would be the primary focus of this mission. In Matthew 25, the Lord talks about judgment and refers to feeding the hungry, giving drink to the thirsty, clothing the naked, helping the sick, visiting prisoners, and showing hospitality to the stranger. Then in Matthews 25:40 He says, "Truly I tell you, whatever you did for one of the least of these brothers and sisters of mine, you did for me." (NIV)

I suppose I had always known about the plight of homeless people. But coming face to face with the suffering they experience and observing the way that they live their daily lives, really had a dramatic impact on me. They, in my opinion, are indeed the "least of these." These are the least cared about, the least able, and possess the least amount of hope for the future—in this world at least. By day three, I realized all of this.

Two really nice homeless travelers pointed us in the direction of Jacksonville, Florida. Apparently, they had recently camped out there for a time. They said that there were tons of homeless in that area, and that we could really make a positive impact. Originally, the plan had been to go to Tampa for our Florida destination, mainly because one of my best friends lived there. It would have been really nice to see him. I had not seen him since his wedding a couple of years prior.

Either unfortunately or fortunately, depending on how you look at it, I had no way of getting in touch with my old Army buddy in Tampa to confirm arrangements or even get his address. I got a good chuckle a few days later when I found out that his daughter had thrown his cell phone into the toilet, which is why we were unable to make contact. Jacksonville was closer to Savannah and our next stop in Alabama. It worked out practically, saving us time and gas. It also worked out spiritually, as we could feel ourselves being called to make the change in destination based on the tip we had from our buddies we made down by the Savannah river walk on day two.

Day three in Jacksonville was one of the most memorable of the trip, as the images from that day still remain quite vivid in my mind. My memory is not as sharp as it once was, not that I am old or broken, but for some reason things just do not seem to stick like they used to. That is not the case with Jacksonville. I will do my best to elaborate on those things, so hopefully you can see them through my eyes, but I am sure that I will be unable to do those experiences justice.

In Jacksonville, I witnessed suffering unlike I had seen before in the United States. We pulled into the city, and it quickly became apparent that the guys in Savannah were right. It seemed as if there was a homeless person camped out in every shade spot you could find. Shopping carts, cardboard, trash, and little makeshift shelters could be seen in all directions it seemed. It was an absolutely miserable, 104-humid degrees without a cloud in the sky. The heat was downright oppressive, and it was impossible not to think about the countless homeless folks that were forced to spend every moment of every day in those conditions.

Our plan of action was to look up homeless shelters on the GPS and start from there. Then we would just figure it out as we went. We found a few shelters in the same part of town, so we figured that this would be the epicenter of our operations for the day. Anytime we could, we would try to partner up with other faith-based operations for reasons that will be displayed later in the story. There was a Christian shelter in the area, so we parked the van and went in to introduce ourselves to the staff on duty. After we gave them a rundown of our mission, and a basic summary of our intentions, they gave us permission to use their parking lot, and the freedom to communicate and minister to folks in and around their facility.

The Dude and I got into our routine, which would become daily practice moving forward. We would read a passage from our daily devotional, pray for the Lord's protection, blessing, and for the guidance and movement of the Holy Spirit. Then we would load up his backpack with cold bottles of water from our cooler and load my rucksack with Bibles and Gospel tracts. Once we collected ourselves, we hit the streets.

I was slapped in the face with suffering almost immediately as there was a double amputee in a wheelchair who looked to be in his 60's or 70's sitting in the direct sunlight on a sidewalk. We spotted him from across the street as we waited for the traffic to clear the intersection so that we could cross. I could not help but notice, not a single person passing by, either walking or driving, even acknowledged that the man was there. It was as if he were invisible to everybody except us.

As we crossed the street, it quickly became apparent to me that this guy was in worse shape than I thought. The poor fellow was passed out, asleep with his chin in his chest, slumped slightly to one side in his wheelchair. His gray sweatpants were darkened in the lap from where the man had urinated on himself, and there were flies collecting on his wet nether regions. Who knows how long he had been wearing those clothes or how long it had been since he had someone who could assist him with a bath?

We did what we could in the moment. The man was breathing normally, and his pulse was strong, so it did not seem like a medical emergency or anything like that. We rolled him into the shade, provided water for when he came to, prayed over him, and if I am not mistaken, we may have gotten another person to wheel him down the road to a place where he could receive some assistance.

I can remember being brought to tears and needing to take a little time to collect myself. I do not know if it was my empathy for this man's suffering or my disgust at the apathy of everyone who passed him by as if he were not there that really upset me the most. Perhaps it was a combination of the two, but the emotions I felt in that moment were a bit overwhelming. As a small-town guy, you just do not come across situations like these every day. I have found that folks who live in large cities and see this type of thing all the time can become desensitized, calloused, and cold-hearted towards the suffering of others. An attitude of, "I can't help everybody, so I might as well not help anybody" seems to take hold of them. We should fight such hard-heartedness at all costs.

Shortly after that, we began to make our way down to the local bus station. It was one of the places we found primed for handing out bookmarks, Bibles, bottles of water, and engaging people in conversation. We found a young man there who looked to be in his early 20's: a lovely soul, with a bright smile that heavily contrasted his very dark skin. I asked him if he had a Bible and offered to give him one if he did not have it already. The young man accepted the book gladly, sat down on a bench, and started to finger through it with a wild curiosity. Our eyes connected as I observed him with joy all over my face. Then He asked me a question that I never could have seen coming: "Did you write this?"

How in the world could anyone in America, the south no less, not know anything about the Bible? It's called the Bible belt for goodness sakes! As someone who had grown up in various churches all my life, seeing them on so many street corners during every drive I had ever taken, it never occurred to me that there were adult Americans who have absolutely no idea about the God and Father of our Lord Jesus Christ. This is a mistake. If you find yourself in service to the Lord, do not make the mistake of assuming that people know the same things you know about the things of God. It does feel awkward; I'm not going to lie to you. No matter how many times you do it, it will always feel a little bit weird talking to complete strangers about Jesus.

This is because the culture and times in which we find ourselves living. There is an established atmosphere where opinions about God can land anywhere on a wide spectrum. There is no way to know where on that spectrum someone is going to land as you approach them. Perhaps they have no idea who Jesus is, or maybe they have a doctorate in theology. They may have been raised in church, but now profess atheism, having lost the faith somewhere along the road of life. They may look like a cold hard thug or a Gothic devil worshiper but inwardly are seeking a relationship with God and meaning in life that comes from something bigger than themselves.

One can make assumptions, but that is basically just profiling based on stereotypes, and will likely cause more problems than good. In fact, this is what the militant non-believer is expecting evangelical Christians to do: tell them how bad they are and throw the Bible at their head. The best way to go about evangelistic endeavors is to start with prayer, depend on the guidance and assistance of the Holy Spirit to open the doors of opportunity, while giving you the words to speak in the time that you need them. There are several places in the Gospels where Jesus tells His disciples not to worry about what they would say in defense of their faith, as they bore witness to His life, death, resurrection, and ascension throughout the ancient world. The Lord promised that the Holy Spirit would give them the words that they needed at the appropriate time. (Luke 12:11-12)

We also must come from a place of absolute humility, realizing that we are only sinners who have been saved by the grace of God, not because we are special or better than anyone else, but because God is loving, merciful, and really freaking cool! We did not earn our salvation; it is a gift from God. (Ephesians 2:8-9) Throughout the Gospels, there is one thing that seems to anger Jesus more than anything else: self-righteousness. The Lord constantly and consistently put the scribes and Pharisees on blast for their self-righteousness in proclaiming that they were better than everyone else because of their strict adherence to the Mosaic Law. Pastor and Evangelist, Greg Laurie, often uses the analogy, "I am not better than anyone else. All I am is just one beggar trying to tell another beggar where to find food." Feel free to check out the words of the Lord, Himself, in Chapter 18 of Luke's Gospel.

The Gospel is the great equalizer. It transcends race, gender, social status, education level, and any other label you can come up with. It levels the playing field for all of us. The Gospel is the same for the prince and the prisoner, for the president and the prostitute, the best of the best, and the worst of the worst. Every single one of us has sinned and fallen short of the Glory of God. (Romans 3:23) This means that every single person would be found guilty, and rightfully so, if we were to come before the righteous judge of all the Earth. This means that we deserve to be punished for the wrongs that we have committed against God and His Creation. The degree of the punishment could be argued about, and surely is debated by theologians and secularists alike. But our guilt in the eyes of a holy and righteous God, in accordance with His written command, is irrefutable.

In Jacksonville, we met people all along the spectrum. On one end there was a fine young man who thought I wrote the Bible, and on the other, a couple of gangsters (the real kind that will shoot you) who doubted that they could be forgiven for the things they had done. We also came across an unsuspecting man who seemed to know the Bible front back and sideways. It seemed as if every single word he spoke throughout our ten-to-fifteen-minute conversation was directly from Scripture. In one day, I had the opportunity to introduce someone to God's Word for the very first time, share my testimony of forgiveness and salvation with two men that desperately needed it, and was blessed immeasurably by one who could have been an angel, or The Lord Himself, for all I know. I do remember being hit with a particular scripture about the incident,

Hebrews 13:2, "Don't forget to show hospitality to strangers, for some who have done this have entertained angels without realizing it." (NLT)

Without a doubt, this man was Christ-like. I've heard someone call it Jesus with skin on. This encounter reminded us of our purpose to make disciples like this man was: people who are so transformed by the Word and spirit of God that when you are around them it is a transformative and almost supernatural experience. We ran into him toward the end of the day, when The Dude and I were physically, mentally, and spiritually exhausted. The boost we received from the time we were with him, and the prayer as we departed each other's company, was undeniable. Like a cold glass of living water after walking through the spiritual desert, we were immeasurably refreshed by the experience.

After walking in the Spirit for a while, you start to realize that there is no randomness, that everything is planned out, and that the timing is impeccable—but only if you are walking in the Spirit. The encounter we had with the man of God was on our walk back to the van, after hoofing it in the hundred-plus sun all day long. If we had let the flesh conquer the Spirit, then we would have given the man a quick hello and a head nod, passing him by, feeling that we had done enough already. But we would have missed out on the refreshment that he gave, in addition to the blessing that was to follow.

Just around the corner from where our spiritual conversation had taken place was the shelter where we had parked the van. As we got inside the parking area and courtyard, there were considerably more people than we had seen before, and more rolling in by the minute. It turned out that this was the time to check in for dinner and to reserve a spot for the night. According to the guy who worked at the shelter, there was only a short window of time, about fifteen minutes, when you could get in, so everybody flooded in at the same time. I suppose it is to avoid folks loitering around outside all day. We were able to distribute a ton of Bibles and encourage a lot of hurting guys who were in line to receive their food and shelter for the night. Had we missed the conversation with that man of God, we would have left the shelter right before the influx and missed the valuable chance to share God's Word with these men. Timing is everything, and when walking in the Spirit, the timing is perfect, because God's time is always the right time.

Chapter 4
Speaking of Timing

After leaving the shelter, we decided to head down the road to Jacksonville Beach. Traveling through forty-eight states in forty-eight days was pretty cool, but we figured that it would also be pretty neat to put our boots in both the Atlantic and Pacific Oceans while making our way across all of the southern states, which would take us coast to coast. We dipped our boots, grabbed some chow, and then started the next leg of the adventure, headed to Alabama.

Fortunately, we were blessed to be able to stay with some wonderful family members of mine near Savannah for the first couple of nights of the mission trip. They were very gracious hosts before and after our stop in that city. They loaded us up with all kinds of supplies that would come in handy as part of God's plan later in the trip. After making the trek from Jacksonville to Montgomery, we had our first van sleeping experience. We were worried that the van might overheat if we ran the air conditioning all night, so we ran it intermittently, cooling the inside of the vehicle to a bearable temperature then turning off the engine. Soon the sticky Alabama heat would cause us to wake up in a pool of our own sweat, and we would repeat the procedure again.

That night also sticks out and causes me to giggle a little. At some point in the night I awoke in a panic, and halfway between dream and reality, it appeared to me that the van was hurling across the parking lot at about thirty-five miles per hour with no one in the driver's seat. I jumped up and crawled frantically across the floor of the van, and in a valiant attempt to stop the vehicle, I dove under the steering wheel pushing down on the brake pedal as hard as I could with both hands. I started to come back to the real world as it clicked in my head that either the brakes were not working or we were not really moving. Both of us being combat vets, The Dude and I had experienced our fair share of vivid nightmares. After the incident we had a good laugh about it.

The next day, we were hot and sweaty but felt rested, nonetheless. We figured that we would start off the day hoofing it through downtown Montgomery, but it was a ghost town. There was not a soul to be found outside on the streets. We deferred back to the strategy of looking for the location of a homeless shelter in the area, thinking perhaps there would be some outreach opportunities around there.

It turned out that, even in that area of the city, nobody was on the streets. I suppose that with the oppressive and humid 100-plus degree midday temperatures, we were the only one's crazy enough to be out there for any substantial amount of time. We decided to go into the shelter and see if maybe they could give us some tips that might point us in the right direction, where we could make the largest ministry impact in their area. It turned out that they were just about to serve lunch at the shelter, and we figured that we would just pitch in as servers and help out for the afternoon. If I remember correctly, they were short staffed for some reason.

There was a clear undeniable tension in the cafeteria from the moment we walked in. The Dude and I were the only white people there, with the exception of one fellow who was just traveling through. I could not remember feeling that much racial tension and hostility in my life. Growing up in the small-town south, I have experienced all kinds of racism. I've heard all the jokes and seen the cliques of separation that date all the way back to the days of segregation. However, I had never felt such an underlying anger by a group as I did that day. I worried that this was just the way that it was in that part of Alabama, and that racial relations in that area were still very rocky, decades behind the progress made in other parts of the urban south.

I actually did not put two and two together until a short time ago, as I was remembering the events of the trip in preparation for writing this story. I thought about the racial tension in Montgomery, and it seemed to click in my head that there must have been more to it than just normal racial tension. I got curious and remembered during that summer a horrendous shooting took place, where a disturbed, young, white man walked into a traditionally black church in Charleston, killing several in a cold-blooded, hate-driven atrocity.

I was right about the connection, and it all made sense, when, after a few seconds of google research, I realized that the shooting had taken place the evening before. The shooting took place on the evening of June 17th, and there we were, two white guys in Team Jesus t-shirts, serving food and washing dishes as humble servants of the Lord, surrounded by a population of ninety-nine percent African-Americans. Towards the end of our time there, the tension and hostility had eased considerably. God undoubtedly arranged the timing of this encounter as we found ourselves at the right place at the right time to be able to make an impact against the evils of hate.

Bad things happen. Sometimes the enemy lands a shot, but in times like that, it is most important to be a force for good. When bad things happen it is imperative that we make some type of positive impact in an attempt to bring at least some good out of the negative situation. Romans 12:21 states, "Do not be overcome by evil but overcome evil with good." We cannot have the attitude of, "it is what it is" when it comes to evil. There is a statement that has often been quoted by John F. Kennedy, Edmond Burke, and others that indeed holds great truth: "The only thing necessary for the triumph of evil is for good men to do nothing." I do not know the real impact we made that day, but I have no doubt that we made an impact for good.

Another instance of God's perfect timing was in Phoenix, Arizona. We had just traveled from Albuquerque, New Mexico where we had a time of fellowship and refreshment in The Dude's old stomping grounds. That also left us battling the flesh as we were enjoying a little bit of relaxation after tearing through the south for the last ten straight days. After staying the night with The Dude's aunt, enjoying a big breakfast, and slowly getting our gear refit inside the van, we shoved out a little later than we had hoped for. To be honest, I was not really looking forward to spending the day in the sweltering Arizona summer sun.

We got into downtown Phoenix in the late afternoon. Not having any plans ironed out for outreach that day, and no real prior knowledge of the city, we rolled in, as we usually did, just trying to find the most people. Often, we would look for parks, bus stations, and city centers where the largest number of people would typically congregate. For some reason, as we entered the city, the GPS navigation system we were using went completely goofy. Right about that time, my leg started to cramp up. Along the inside and outside of my lower legs I have scars from the bilateral fasciotomies that the surgeons performed on me after I was blown up. Apparently, if they did not cut open my legs on both sides, they would pop like a hotdog in a microwave due to the trauma of the explosion. It was not a new thing, and it usually did not bother me that much. But this time was different. It got so bad that I could no longer drive for fear that I was going to have an accident in the five o'clock traffic we were trying to navigate.

We had to pull off to the side of the road and regroup. It was clear that we needed the Lord's help, and for one reason or another, things simply were not going in our favor. We prayed, asking for the Lord's guidance as to what we should do next. We asked the question: what good can we do in this city? The van was cluttered and crowded with goods that sweet people along the way had given us for the trip. There were some non-perishable food items like crackers, fruit cups, and little boxes of cereal that were taking up a lot of space. When we were on foot away from the van, we really only had room for Bibles and water, and the food would most likely get damaged or wet if we tried to carry it with us.

We decided that we would find a local shelter and donate the food to them; they would surely be able to put it to good use. As we pulled up beside the shelter, there was a gentleman who seemed to be waiting for us. As soon as we got out of the van, the man, Rey, was eager to help us out. You never really knew what to expect when being approached by a stranger, especially in an area of town with a lot of people living on the streets, but this guy was solid gold. He greeted us with a joyful smile and some corny Christian jokes that lifted our spirits. For instance: how did Jesus and all His disciples get around? In one accord! LOL.

After taking the food inside the shelter, we started to think about what our next move would be. Rey continued to hang out with us, shooting the breeze as we prepped our packs. We figured we would head out on foot and see what we could accomplish in the next few hours before the sunset. As soon as we got to the sidewalk, we looked to the right and witnessed a mass exodus of homeless people headed right for us. The sidewalk on both sides of the street was packed for almost as far as the eye could see. For a second, I thought that we were in the path of some type of protest or demonstration. We inquired from Rey what was going on, and he told us that down the road was the dinner shelter, and after eating chow many of the city's homeless would come to this overnight shelter in hopes of reserving a place to sleep for the night.

Once again, we found ourselves in the right place at the right time. In a very short period, we were able to distribute gallons of refreshing water, every pack of crackers we had, and, thanks to Rey, thirty-two Bibles and over a hundred Gospel tracts. We even had the opportunity to pray with thirty-five people. On a day when we could not find our way, and my legs were probably too beat up to walk very far, God brought the people to us, and even had a servant waiting there to help.

There was no way that we could have possibly had anything to do with the success of the mission that day. It was completely and totally arranged by God. All we had to do was pray that God would move and then be available to serve. As I think back on the events of that day, I think of the words of the Lord in Matthew 9:36-38, "When he saw the crowds, he had compassion on them, because they were harassed and helpless, like sheep without a shepherd. Then he said to his disciples, 'The harvest is plentiful but the workers are few. Ask the Lord of the harvest, therefore, to send out workers into his harvest field.'" (NIV)

Chapter 5
The Way Jesus Did It

Days like we had in Phoenix, when we were given the opportunity to make an impact with a large group of people, were always a blessing, but I still feel that nothing compares to the one-on-one and small-group interactions that took place on the trip. The numbers are cool, tangible evidence that confirms what we were accomplishing, but nothing was more important than the intangible impact made when we invested in an individual soul. Jesus focused on both. There is not only the Sermon on the Mount, but also the woman at the well. He not only fed the multitudes, but also sat with His disciples regularly to teach them the mysteries of the faith. He not only preached at the Temple and synagogues, but also met with Nicodemus in the quiet of the night.

For us, it was very much the same. There were the days when we would hand out hundreds of bookmarks and tracts on Bourbon Street, the Vegas Strip, or in front of a pro baseball stadium, but the blessing of deep and meaningful fellowship with individuals was always greater. Many people think that speaking in front of crowds is difficult, but I think that the most challenging part of the Great Commission is intimate conversation: the uncomfortable nature of being in a foreign environment with a complete stranger, being secure enough in your beliefs to engage on the ground level, willing to face any opposing thought or opinion. It makes the biggest impact, because it is the toughest thing to do.

Another factor that makes that type of ministry difficult are the barriers. That type of one-on-one ministry will require you to spend time with the very type of people who, if you were raised in church culture, you have been told over and over again not to hang around with. But once again I am reminded of Jesus' encounter with the woman at the well for the reason why this is so important. There were multiple religious and societal barriers that were destroyed by

Jesus in that one exchange. In fact, even His disciples were taken aback by the encounter. First, we have a Jew conversing with a Samaritan, which was a real no-go in the culture at the time. Outside of that, we have a Rabbi spending time with a woman; another cultural faux pas, and not just any woman, an adulterous woman who had been married five times and was currently living out of wedlock with her bedmate. As it turns out, that woman would be the witness who would take her testimony of Jesus back to her village, resulting in the belief and salvation of many.

We must not be afraid to get our hands dirty. We must put our boots on the ground, meeting people *where* they are and *how* they are. The Apostle Paul talked about that in the sixth chapter of his letter to the church in Ephesus. He called it the full armor of God. I like to think of it as a scuba suit. Scuba divers put on wet suits, masks, and goggles so they can enter into the depths of the sea without being affected by the water. We can also achieve this by being firmly rooted in our salvation, having spent considerable time with God, nourished by His Word and His Spirit. Then, we can be in the world but not of the world, affecting it but not being influenced and corrupted by it. In this chapter of the story, I want to focus on those conversations, tell you the people's stories, and bestow upon you the lessons that I have learned from them.

In New Orleans, we spent the whole day walking up and down Bourbon street in the hot sun, surrounded by all things sinful, yet attempting to be a positive influence for the Lord. We handed out hundreds of bookmarks and gospel tracts that day, but the highlight of the day for me was the time spent with a homeless, broken drunk on the steps of a monument near the mighty Mississippi. At first, he just wanted some food and water, seeming quite skeptical and a little intimidating. I had to fight the temptation to get on the road, feeling that we had accomplished enough that day, and anticipating the pressing weight of another long drive awaiting us that evening. However, when we dropped the food and

111

water off for this man, I could hear that Still Small Voice telling me to take the time to sit beside him and talk for a while.

Our conversation started off very superficial—small talk. Then, as he became more comfortable with me, his guard began to drop, and we were able to get into deeper conversation. He would soon begin to tell me his story, and how he had ended up in the situation where I found him. The man confided in me that he had done a long stint in prison for killing his own brother. I did not pass any judgment on him; instead, I chose to just listen and keep him company for the moment as he poured out his heart and soul. Apparently, the man had walked into his house after work one night to find that his wife and child had been brutally murdered by his brother who had recently returned from the Persian Gulf conflict in the early 90's. After walking into the horrific scene and discovering his brother still present with their blood on his hands, in a rage, he took his brother's life.

As he broke down sobbing, I could feel the tremendous pangs of empathy for this poor broken man. I shared with him how I, too, had taken life, how it haunted me for years, and that the only thing that had brought me comfort was my relationship with Jesus Christ. I told him that Jesus' sacrifice was big enough to cover all of our sins, if we are willing to confess them to God and ask for forgiveness. I told him that we cannot change the past, and that what is done is done, but God can change our future, and can use those terrible things for good. I asked him if he was ready for a fresh start, a new life in Christ. We prayed together and cried together, and at the end of it, as the sun began to set, we each felt a tremendous peace come over us, as if the very Spirit of God had enveloped us. The time had come for The Dude and me to shove off to the next location. I handed the man a Bible and had to trust that God would continue His redemptive work in the man's life.

That is another difficult part of boots-on-the-ground ministry—having to leave it in the hands of the Lord, trusting that His Spirit will complete the good work. In Chapter 4 of John's

Gospel, Jesus talks about planting and harvesting. Sometimes it is our job to plant and sometimes to harvest—rarely do we know which of the two before it happens. Much of the time, we found ourselves planting seeds like that day on Bourbon street, but occasionally we had the beautiful pleasure of being able to take part in the harvest, when after considerable time of wrestling with God, someone was finally ready to lay down their arms in submitting their life and will to Christ.

In both circumstances, the planting and the harvesting, we must remember that salvation is the work of the Spirit. No matter how much effort and time we put in, how articulately we speak, how persuasive our arguments, it is God who does the saving—not us. God has set it up this way. In order to be fruitful as believers, we must be in fellowship with Him. Jesus described it as the relationship between a vine and its branches. He is the vine, and we are the branches. We receive our life, strength, and spiritual power from Him through fellowship with Him. If a branch is separated from the vine, then it will wither and die. The same is true of us. Apart from Him, in our own strength, we are fruitless and worthless to the kingdom. Salvation is a gift from God, and none of us can take credit for it.

Love—deep, unconditional, agape love—is the key to making a lasting impact in the lives of people. Paul talks about that in 1 Corinthians 13. Love is the greatest of all virtues and holds them all together. If we do not have love, then everything we do is worthless. Radical love does not make sense to those who are of this world, because it is selfless and often sacrificial in nature. Jesus said, "Greater love has no one than this: to lay down one's life for his friends." (John 15:13 NIV) This type of sacrificial love is what the Gospel is all about, and indwelling in us is the transformational power that changes lives. It brings to mind a part of our journey, when I met a drug dealer in Minneapolis, Minnesota.

As we came into the city, we once again did not have a solid plan for where we would operate that day. We checked out a few parks looking for groups of people that we could minister to and really had no luck, other than stumbling across what appeared to be some type of Muslim rally. At first, I felt the pull towards confrontation, thinking that perhaps our purpose was to get into a heated theological discussion with the goal of setting them straight, but that was not the case with Jesus. If someone confronted Him, He would gladly drop a truth bomb on them, but you do not see Him out looking for a fight.

We kept driving until we found a large homeless shelter nestled in what appeared to be an abandoned section of the city. It was similar to the Wild West in some aspects. There were surveillance cameras set up in various places, but in the several hours we were there, I did not see one patrol car or any type of police presence other than a guy walking around in a sheriff t-shirt, who was obviously not an elected civic leader, if you catch my drift. When we first arrived there were probably about thirty people who had started to gather on the block near the shelter. I would say that five or six of those folks were drug dealers, lookouts, or somewhere in between. There were various deals happening all around, and there were even some females there who would sneak off between the buildings and sell their bodies. Many "church people" would never set foot in a place like this and, as a result, miss the greatest of opportunities.

We began our normal routine of distributing water, granola bars, and Gospel tracts among the people we saw there, homeless and dealers alike. We displayed no prejudice, picked no favorites, and just treated everybody as if they were the most important person in the world. As we were talking and praying with folks, a loud altercation at the end of the road grabbed my attention. Apparently one of the dealers had come into contact with a user who had not yet paid for his last transaction. Anyone who has any type of experience in a situation like this can tell you that being in debt to a drug dealer is not where you want to be. I hear, "Where's my m****** f****** money?!" The fellow replies, "I'm gonna get it, I promise." The

114

dealer replies "Oh, you gonna get it alright. I'm gonna go to my car and get my heat, and if I don't have my money today, oh you gonna get it!" To me this was a clear threat on the man's life.

I could feel the Spirit urging me to take some type of action. Should I go talk to the dealer and let him know that this is not the way? Should I call the cops? Would they even care? Plus, this is not the part of town where you want to be snitching on people. Then it hit me out of nowhere. I knew what to do! I found one of the dope boys and pulled him to the side to chat. I asked the dope boy if he knew the dealer that was involved in the shouting match with the addict. He replied that he did. I said to him, "Can you find out how much he owes?" The young man was clearly taken aback. His reply was "Why you wanna know?" I simply stated that I wanted to pay the man's debt so that he would not get hurt, but I needed to find out how much so that I could make sure that I had enough to cover it.

Reluctantly, the young man went to his guy so that he could bring me back a number: twenty-five dollars. That's right folks. You can get shot over a twenty-five-dollar drug debt, if you were not already aware of that. Your life in the streets is probably not nearly as valuable as you think it is. I told him that once things settled down and we went back to the van to refit, I would get it for him. About twenty minutes later I made good on my word. In fact, I gave him twenty-seven dollars just to make sure.

His mind was blown. It was easy to see that he had never experienced anything like that before—a complete stranger, from across the country, offering to pay the bad debt of a drug addict. In fact, he even said so. He said, "I ain't never seen nothing like this." Then came my window to share the gospel. He said, "Why you doing this?" I told him that I had a debt that I could not pay, but Jesus paid my debt for me, the debt of my sin. I shared with him some of my history of running from God, the partying, the drugs, the people I had hurt, and the people I had killed in combat. The price was too high for me to pay to be right with God after all the things I had done, but Jesus paid that price on the Cross for me. That was why I wanted to pay that man's debt and to help everybody I can while I can. Jesus had changed me.

I told the young man that Jesus could do the same thing for him, too, and that this life he was living was not all there is. I told him that God had bigger plans for him than standing on this street corner. He had to get back to what he was doing, but I could tell that something had struck a chord within his soul. As the sun set, and we started to pack up shop, the young man approached me and said, "Hey, you got another one of them Bibles?" Praise the Lord! All I can hope is that he did indeed turn to the Lord, and now several years later, finds himself on a higher path.

I cannot remember all of the people we handed a Bible too, but there was one young lady who received one, and I am almost brought to tears thinking about her. When The Dude and I were in Salt Lake City, we came across a park that was literally packed with homeless people. It was like a playground for people whom society had forgotten; they had been left in this place as a sanctuary to exist however they saw fit. Within just a few moments of walking onto the scene, we saw the rampant use of hard drugs.

The first folks that we walked up to were noticeably standoffish and clearly strung out on something; my guess was heroin or pills. Those folks fit firmly into the category of people whom we, unfortunately, encountered a lot—people who had become so deep in their addiction that they had left society behind. They had left behind family, careers, dreams, religion, friends, and anything else that mattered to live a life that revolved solely around getting their fix. There were no conversations, no prayer requests. They did not even really seem thankful for the cold water on a hot day. We gave them a couple of bookmarks with the waters but felt quite unwelcome, and with so many others to minister to in the park, we gave them a blessing and moved on. We tried our best to first make our rounds distributing food and water to everyone in the park where there must have been more than a hundred people at least.

116

Then we circled back to talk to the folks who seemed most receptive, trying to distribute some Bibles and engaging them in conversation.

There was a group of Ugandan and Sudanese refugees who had fled their war-torn countries in search of something better. We really connected with them as we found out that they, too, were mostly veterans of some type of conflict. As we would find out, many of them had a deep love for Jesus. There is something magical about the feeling of coming together in fellowship with other true believers who love Christ. We were both energized and encouraged by the encounter. I will talk more about fellowship and friends a little later, but I am sure of the Scripture when Jesus said, "Where two or three gather in my name, there am I with them." (Matthew 18:20 NIV)

We made our second round in the park, talking to various folks, handing out additional water where needed, trying to pray with as many people as we could, and hand out Bibles to anyone willing to accept one. Eventually, the supplies started to dwindle, and the sun began to settle for the night as darkness crept in slowly from the East. It was once again time to wrap it up and get on the road. On our way out, we walked by the area where the first group of standoffish addicts had been. Now there was only one girl seated there, as the others had headed off to do what they needed to do to prepare for the evening's activities. She was an attractive and seemingly intelligent young lady who looked to be around twenty years old. I could not help but wonder how she had ended up there. I did not ask. Some questions can be painful and do more harm than good. She asked if we had any more food and water.

I went to the van, maybe just twenty yards away, and grabbed the last few waters we had and some Meals Ready to Eat (MREs) that we had been hanging onto. Remembering that she was originally part of a group of about four or five, I made sure she had enough food to share whenever they returned. As I delivered the food and turned to walk away, the young lady made a statement that broke my heart and stopped me dead in my tracks. She said, "Thanks

117

for trying to help a drug addict piece of trash like me." I instantly felt like fighting, like I had been shot at, like I had seen someone slap my mama! I felt that the enemy, the evil one, had been having his way with this poor girl, and I was there for the sole purpose of fighting on God's behalf.

"No, no, no, no, no, please don't say that," I told her, in a soft and broken-hearted tone. Kneeling beside her, I did not even give her a chance to defend her statement of self-loathing. I told her that she is valuable, not a piece of trash, and that God thinks that she's worth dying for, worth sending His Son to die for. I told her that God loved her more than she could possibly imagine, and that this is not who she is, but instead, just where she is at. I could not fight the imposing thought that this was someone's daughter; in a few years it could be my daughter. I had to start fighting tears and trying to talk through the lump in my throat. Placing a Bible on the ground next to her, I let her know that Jesus loves her and wants to have a relationship with her, to take her from where she is to where she should be. God wants to be your Heavenly Father and give you the life you were created for. It was true for her, and it's true for you, too.

Chapter 6
Expect Opposition

One of the scariest moments of my life, when I felt that I would not see the sunrise the next day, was April 9, 2004. I was on my first deployment to Iraq and had only been in the country for a short time. Our mission had been fairly relaxed and uneventful up to that point, as I remember it. There was no contact as we drove in from Kuwait for hours that seemed as if they would never end. Sure, we had been mortared a little on the Forward Operating Base (FOB) and heard a few pop shots here and there, as well as the sound of IED's exploding in the distance. It was nothing worth writing home about but enough to serve as a constant reminder that death was out there, waiting.

If I am not mistaken, it was Good Friday, and as the city began to fill with the noise of gunfire and muffled explosions, it sounded almost like a big sporting event. It ebbed and flowed, like the tide of momentum in a basketball game, going from a low hum to boisterous applause when the home team drained a three or scored a big dunk. It was apparent while listening to the radio that there was fighting all over the city. It seemed that every patrol was taking some kind of contact. Police stations were being taken over by hostile militia fighters who had infiltrated the city. For some reason, we did not go out that day. Perhaps, they wanted us to stay back for the security of the FOB, so that it would not get overrun if things went from bad to worse.

As evening arrived, we began to see a lot of the other platoons come in from the fighting for brief respites while they grabbed some chow, rehydrated, refueled, reloaded, reequipped, and prepared to continue the fight into the night. Once darkness set in, there was a time when the sounds of the crowd settled and the usual pop shots here and there were all that could be heard. Halftime. The sounds of conflict all over the city would soon be heard again as both parties gained their second wind. Then we got the call to report to Battalion Headquarters for our mission brief.

The Bull, our Battalion Commander, was a tremendous man, not only of stature, but also in presence. He gave us the brief, and never before had I heard anything so direct or piercing in my life. He said, "All routes are black. You will come into contact. It is not a matter of if but when. The Bradley's are running low on ammo, and we do not have any here to resupply them with. I need you to drive across the city, pick up a truck load of ammo from the other FOB, and bring it back." Petrified, I always knew that we were in a combat zone and that at some point in time things were going to happen, but being told that this was the moment changed my whole mindset. A fear sank deep into my soul as I thought that this may be the end of my life. Not even a full year had passed since I was sitting in a high school classroom, riding around looking for a party, bird-dogging chicks, just chasing the next good feeling, and now I was going to die in a foreign country before my life even had any meaning at all.

I have come to learn that mindset is everything. Chuck Swindoll is a great preacher whom I like to listen to occasionally on the radio. He said, "Life is ten percent what happens to you and ninety percent how you deal with it." I have told many of my soldiers, guys that I have trained, that there is an attitude that you must have about combat. Please pardon my language, but I must give it to you the same way I gave it to them; "There are only two ways to look at it: either I hope a m*****f**** don't, or I wish a m****f**** would." I learned this lesson on April 9th.

After being shocked to the core by the mission brief that we had received, I probably tried not to show it, but behind the façade of cockiness and portrayed readiness, I was terrified and most likely would have run away if there had been anywhere to go. As we rolled out the gate and locked and loaded our weapons, we knew that there was no turning back, no order to turn around being issued from the Tactical Operations Center (TOC)—it was on!

120

To be honest, I had the attitude of hoping that nothing happened, that somehow maybe the colonel was wrong, and we would just have a fear filled, extremely nerve-wracking trip across the city and back that proved to be uneventful. I can remember praying the whole time, and looking back, it's funny how all you can think about is God when you think you are going to die. Even now as I am writing this, I feel myself holding my breath in anticipation of what was to come. In the back of an unarmored Humvee, ratchet strapped to a 50-caliber machine gun on a pole, completely exposed to any and all enemy fire, God was the only hope I had as we sped through the middle of the city. Seeing the buildings grow larger and denser all around us, it felt as if the city was going to swallow us, hopefully to spit us out on the other side.

It started with a small explosion at the front of the convoy, then several more explosions near the second truck, and then around my own. This was followed by small-arms fire so intense that the only thing I could compare it to would be a strand of those firecrackers you get on the Fourth of July that come in a roll of several hundred. You just light the green main fuse and then there they go. There were so many tracers bouncing off the road and buildings that it looked like the laser cannons from Star Wars. I could not even begin to identify a person to shoot at. I didn't know where to start. I froze. I never even fired a shot. I dug my chin into my chest, gritted my teeth, and prayed that we would be able to drive out of it soon, while the whole time anticipating that I would begin to feel the heat of bullets as they rip through my flesh at any given moment.

I still do not know how I did not get hit that night; only God knows. However, I do know that I was completely ineffective and useless, and to this day, I bear some shame that I froze. Had anyone from our platoon died that night, the guilt would have been almost too much to bear. Because I had the attitude of hoping that nothing would happen, when it did, I was not prepared for it. We limped into the other FOB, where we needed to pick up the ammo and spent the next couple of hours loading it and repairing our vehicles. We had numerous flat tires, various leaks in radiators, and other issues because of the fire our trucks had sustained.

When we left to return back to our base, I was ready. I had seen what the enemy had to offer, trusted in the protection that God had provided, and decided that when the enemy attacked again, I would not freeze; I would fight. I welcomed it and anxiously awaited the opportunity to redeem myself. I wished they would just fire and get it over with already so I could let them have it. My attitude change made all the difference. When the contact came this time, I was a different person. The fear that had stopped me dead in my tracks before was no longer present, and I was free to engage the enemy with my weapon. However, there was an issue. Even though I had the right mindset to dig up the courage it takes to pull the trigger, my weapon malfunctioned. The timing on my .50-cal. machine gun was off, and every few shots, it would jam up. This made me much less effective than I would have been if I had properly maintained my weapon. The same is true of Christian warfare in the spiritual realm, but instead of a .50-cal., the weapon is the Word of God.

In Chapter 6 of Paul's letter to the Ephesians, he talks about the full armor of God in the spiritual battle, which all of us happen to be engaged in, whether we believe it or not. There is the belt of truth, which keeps us from getting caught with our pants down. There is the shield of faith, the breastplate of righteousness, the helmet of salvation, and even a pair of shoes. However, the only offensive weapon in the battle-dress uniform for combat in Heaven is the "Sword of the Spirit, which is the Word of God." (Eph. 6:17 NIV) I can tell you this much: if you are going to attempt to serve the Lord, you are going to have to keep your weapon sharp. No matter how much armor you have, if you do not fight back, eventually, the enemy will overcome you.

I cannot express to you how thankful I am for the many hours of Bible study that I put in prior to this mission trip. To be honest, what I have gained from reading God's Word through eyes of faith is immeasurable. It is life-saving and life-sustaining. If you are trying to survive on the battlefield of life without it, you may avoid bullets and be able to take the shots for a while, but eventually, you will succumb to the withering fire both internally, from within your mind, and externally, in the form of other people and circumstances that are within and outside of your control. Imagine a soldier running around on the battlefield unarmed. Though he may have all the armor in the world to protect him, he will never conquer the enemy. All he can do is hope that they run out of bullets and bombs before he can finally take no more.

A professing Christian who does not know the Word of God is like the guy that rides around in the caged golf cart at the driving range picking up balls. Sure, he is doing a lot better than if he were in a normal golf cart or walking around on foot, but he is still the target of every shot that the weekend duffers fire off in the contest of who can hit the ball fetcher. Now, imagine if you will, that the ball fetcher busted out a paintball gun and started to fire retaliatory shots at the golfers. That would be a game changer. That is what knowledge of God's Word does for us. It strengthens our full armor of protection and also gives us the ability to fight offensively against the forces that would oppose us.

There will be opposition. I say again, if you try to do anything meaningful for the Lord, there will be opposition. Without the full armor of God, especially the Sword of the Spirit—the Word of God—you will be defeated. The mission trip was filled with periodic opposition of all shapes and sizes. There were the naysayers, who attempted to kill the idea before it even became reality. They said it was not possible, that any number of things could go wrong and cause the whole mission to be an epic failure. The "what ifs" inside our heads got rolling, and all of a sudden, fifteen worst case scenarios were bouncing through our skulls, but then faith in the Word of God pulled us through. I remembered my command to go according to the Great Commission, and that the

Lord would be with me. I certainly would not know that truth if I had not read it from the book of Matthew many times. The knowledge of the Word of God when put into action by faith makes all the difference in the world. We extinguish the fiery arrows of doubt and then strike back with our all-powerful weapon.

The day before we were set to leave on the mission trip, our faith and resolve were tested. Though we had raised enough funds to cover the entire fifty-day rental of the U-Haul, they told us that we could not rent it for that length of time without a credit card. This would have been a helpful piece of information to know in the three previous visits I had made to their office while making the arrangements. There we were, less than twenty-four hours away from rolling out on a mission trip to which tons of people had donated to help make happen, and it was all going to be derailed because I didn't have a credit card. The Dude and I got frustrated at first, as we could feel the walls closing in on us. I had no idea what to do, so we went out to the truck and prayed. We spilled it out to God that we did not know what to do; we knew He wanted us to do this, but it seemed like everything was going wrong; we needed help. We quoted His promises from the Gospels, saying that anything we ask in His Name will be done for us.

Not long after that, perhaps just minutes after, I got a call from my grandparents asking how things were going. I told them what we were up against, and they quickly and nonchalantly said, "Oh, we have a credit card you can use." I never even thought of asking them for help, but God did His thing. We prayed, and He showed up to make good on His promise. God delivered us time and time again from any and all types of opposition. He never promised that it would be easy. In fact, He said the very opposite. In John 16:33 Jesus said, "I have told you these things, so that in Me you may have peace. In this world you will have trouble. But take heart! I have overcome the world." (NIV)

On the mission there was indeed trouble from time to time, but God was faithful. I think of the time in Jackson, Mississippi when three police cars swooped in on us right outside the VA medical facility. We were praying with our fellow veterans and would offer them a tract or a Bible before they went inside for whatever medical or mental health need had brought them to the facility that day. Apparently, this warranted the attention of the police. They said that we were not allowed to hand out any type of literature on Federal property—which is proselytizing, I guess. I never heard that word before, but I suppose we were guilty of it. We explained that we were both Purple Heart veterans who simply want to minister to our brothers and sisters in arms. We could see that they were becoming more tense as we talked, and they started asking questions about where we had parked and where we were from. I realized that we needed to wave the white flag and concede defeat, choosing to make a hasty retreat.

In Little Rock, Arkansas, a woman who was screaming at the top of her lungs that we were false prophets greeted us as soon as we parked the van. Talk about a rough start to your day of ministry! In Oklahoma City, someone threatened to pull a pistol on us. Drug dealers let us know that our presence was not welcome on their turf. Several Muslims threatened us once the arguments reached a high enough level of intensity. People would walk up and interrupt us in the middle of conversations with others to argue our views, question our motives, or to hurl accusations at us. Some would laugh at us or attempt to get us angry so they could show how Christian we weren't. In Seattle, we even had a grown man in a blue Cookie Monster pajama onesie walking down the street behind us, blaspheming Jesus and shouting all kinds of obscenities.

Here's the deal. I am going to fill you in on a little secret. Even after you know the secret, the battle will not get any easier, but you will be more informed and more prepared to fight against it. I may have already mentioned it, but it is worth mentioning again and again until it sinks in. The first goal of the enemy, Satan, is to keep you from attaining the free gift that God has offered: the salvation of your soul and relationship with Him through faith in His Son

125

Jesus. Once that battle has been lost, the next objective of the enemy is to cause you to be a fruitless believer who accomplishes as little as possible for the Kingdom of God. The demons can no longer have you, but they will do whatever they can to keep you from helping to save others. I have found that there are many external circumstances that can definitely have an effect, but the conflict is waged primarily on the battlefield of the mind.

I will be completely honest; I have fallen victim to these tactics and continue to regularly. It has been weeks since I have been able to write in this book. Sharing this story is the primary objective that God has me working on right now, but it has been almost a month since I have touched it. Why? I have plenty of excuses, some of them good ones. I have three kids, a marriage, a home, vehicles, property, bills, and many other obligations and responsibilities that demand my attention. I am in a management position at my company, directly responsible for fifteen staff members and day-to-day operations. I am already up to my ears in ministry opportunities. The list goes on and on.

In reality, none of these things hold me back from doing what God is telling me to do. I do. The battle is for my mind, my attention. I could wake up an hour earlier than I already do, but I need my sleep (insert whiny tone). I could write in the evening after the kids go to bed. My rationalization is that I need to be in the correct mindset to write, and in the evening, I am tired or burnt out. Truth, I don't feel like it and would rather do something else. As long as I am putting other things—even good things—before my primary mission, then the enemy is winning. In the past month I have not written in this book, but I have watched plenty of YouTube videos. They may have been good videos, not filth or a complete waste of time, but still distracted me from the primary objective. Guess what? Life is tough, and if you do not deliberately invest your time, it will get spent for you and usually not where or how it should be. Manage what you can manage and steward it the way God wants you to. I am telling this to not only *you*, but also *myself.* Defeating the enemy is tough enough; don't make things any easier for him.

Jesus said in Matthew 6:31-33, "So do not worry, saying, 'What shall we eat?' Or 'What shall we drink?' Or 'What shall we wear?' For the pagans run after all of these things, and your Heavenly Father knows that you need them. But seek first His Kingdom and His Righteousness, and all of these things will be given to you as well." (NIV) First things first; this is not just a spiritual principle; it applies to all aspects of successful living. In our walk with God, it is absolutely imperative to discipleship. You can't be a disciple without discipline. It's not a coincidence that those two words look the same.

I can remember seeing a demonstration that effectively demonstrated the point I am trying to make about prioritizing the most important things in life. I will try to explain it in a way that you can visualize it. Feel free to try the demonstration yourself to see that I am not just blowing smoke. I do not know where this originates or who came up with it, but if I did, I would give them the credit.

You're going to need two large glass jars that you can see through. You will also need three large stones, a bunch of small rocks or pebbles, and some sand. It is a two-part demonstration, the first illustrating how your life works out if you do not prioritize things the right way. In the first jar, pour in the sand. This represents the unnecessary things that distract and occupy our time, like television, video games, social media, and other time-wasters. Then pour in the smaller rocks and pebbles, they represent the things that need to be done, but are not the most important. These are things like laundry, mowing the grass, paying bills, walking the dog, and taking a shower. They are time occupiers. Unlike the sand, they are necessary, but not of the utmost importance or priority level in our lives. Lastly, attempt to put in the three big stones. These represent the three most important areas of our lives: faith, family, and work. When you put in the sand and pebbles first, there is only room for maybe one large stone, and for most of us, this is probably the work stone. This leaves us in a situation where all our time is occupied or wasted with the little things, and the super important matters of faith and family are neglected entirely.

When we put the items in opposite order, it changes the entire dynamic. The second jar is the exact same size as the first, but this time, we are going to put the first things first. Our three big stones will be placed in the jar first. Then pour in the small stones and follow that up with the sand. To your amazement, and to any others who are observing, it all fits now. When we prioritize the important things first, our faith, family, and careers will flourish and prosper, each having a dramatic effect on the others. We still have the time to do all of the little "must dos" that are represented in the small stones, and at the end of the day, there will also be time for a little sand.

The main point of this exercise is to show that everyone has the same amount of time in the day; it is all a matter of how we use it. If you prioritize the time in the wrong way, then there will not be enough time for the things that really matter, and the consequences of this are often quite painful. However, if we intentionally prioritize our time in accordance with our highest values, if anything does get left out, it doesn't really matter that much. "Oh poop, I didn't get to play video games today because I was studying my Bible, writing a book, working in the yard with my family, and planning the next staff meeting." That is a lot easier to swallow than, "I am going through a divorce, got overlooked for a promotion, and don't really know what I believe anymore, but I am ranked thirty-seventh in the world on this first-person shooter."

I know I am beating this to death, but time is our most valuable asset. The devil wants to occupy your mind and steal your time so that it cannot be invested properly. Most of us, especially me, are our own worst enemies because we choose comfort over priority. We take the path of least resistance. In Matthew Chapter 7:13-14, Jesus says, "Enter through the narrow gate. For wide is the gate and broad is the road that leads to destruction, and many enter through it. But small is the gate and narrow the road that leads to life, and only a few find it." (NIV) The enemy is good at what he does; don't help him out.

I will share something with you that I have not told anyone until now. There were four distinct days of personal weakness that took place in the mission trip about which I still feel guilty. They were the days when fatigue, laziness, disdain, and other emotions led me to fail. In Montana, we were absolutely wiped out. We had just finished a twelve-hour driving stretch from Seattle, Washington. We did absolutely zero outreach in that city. We decided to go to a local park and throw the baseball around for a while, prior to riding to the local Applebee's for a fancy sit down dinner. Some may say, "Oh, well you needed a break after three solid weeks of traveling and outreach." Perhaps they are right, but perhaps, I missed the opportunity to have a conversation or pray with someone going through an awful situation resulting in their life being changed forever. Only God knows the answer.

North Dakota was a completely different circumstance but a similar result. When we pulled into Fargo, it was being drenched with a consistent steady downpour that showed no signs of letting up any time soon. In accordance with our usual routine of purchasing water and granola bars in preparation of the day's activities, I pulled into the local super store. The Dude was still sleeping, so I figured I would grab a haircut and get some breakfast chow from Subway. We were just a few days away from Illinois where my wife and children were staying at her parent's house. I wanted to make sure that I looked presentable when I saw her. Then I had a brilliant idea: *why don't we just keep driving to Minneapolis where it's not raining and get a day ahead on the schedule? Then we can get a full day of R&R at my in-laws' house, and I will get to spend some more time with my wife and kids. It will be great!*

But what was missed? I have the rest of my life to spend with my wife and kids. I may never be in Fargo, North Dakota again.

What if I had a Bible that was meant to get into the hands of the next Billy Graham there in that city on that day. Once again, only God knows. God was gracious to give us an amazing afternoon in Minneapolis, but the day of R&R was anything but. The free night that was afforded by just driving through Fargo, instead of spending the day there, is probably the biggest regret of the whole trip. My wife and I got a motel room when we stopped in her hometown. I drank that night, which I should never do, and feel horrible about it still. I had the worst night sleep I have ever had. Keep in mind, I have had some pretty crappy nights. I felt absolutely terrible about the fact that I had fallen into temptation the way that I did. Here I am representing Christ in a nationwide outreach and getting drunk at a bar.

Recently, I have been doing a Bible study plan that was developed by Francis Chan, a great Christian teacher, and I highly recommend that you check him out. It is a study of the book of James. James, who is thought to be the brother of Jesus, addresses both of these issues in his writings. First, he talks about temptation; "When tempted, no one should say, 'God is tempting me.' For God cannot be tempted by evil, nor does he tempt anyone; but each person is tempted when they are dragged away by their own evil desire and enticed." (James 1:13-14 NIV) The temptation is not always black and white. It's not always distinguishable and can be camouflaged as a good thing. It comes from our flesh, our selfish desires. We must ask the question always: *is this what God wants or what I want?*

I break down sin into two basic categories, sins of commission and sins of omission. The sins of commission are the things that we do that we know we shouldn't do, or rather that God commands us not to do. Most folks have a good grasp on these. My sin of commission was that I got drunk and dishonored Christ.

The sins of omission are a little bit trickier, and I think that these are perhaps the most dangerous because we are never really aware of the consequences, or we fail to make the connection. In this circumstance, my sin of omission was passing through Fargo without doing outreach so that we could get ahead of schedule—my own selfish desire for time off and a brief respite of pleasure. One known consequence was that it set the stage for my sin of commission, but the other consequences will be known only in eternity.

I think that because there are these two distinct types of sin, there will be a much different form of judgment than most people think. Most folks think about judgment as God putting you on blast for all the things you did wrong in your life, like a cosmic principal who used to be a drill sergeant and called you into his office. I think that there will be some of that, because otherwise God would not be righteous and just, but I also think that there will be a part where God reveals to someone what could have been but was squandered.

The fact of the matter is that there will be opposition. It will come from inside and outside of you, but God's grace is sufficient. He will be enough. Do your part, and trust that God will handle the things you can't. I like to think of it as "Do your best, and let God do the rest." When I played football in high school, I gave my absolute best effort on every single play of every single game. Whether we won or lost, I did not want to look back and say that I could have tried harder.

There are a lot of things in this life that are out of our control, and we must trust God with those things, pray about those things, and then fling them at the feet of Jesus as an offering for Him to handle. Effort is always under our control. Some may be smarter, stronger, better looking, come from a better family background, and have more money. We are not all equal, no matter how much people would like that to be so, but you can always be the hardest worker in the room.

By setting our priorities straight, we can focus our efforts. Our efforts can then be used and blessed by God for His greater purposes. Remember the story in the Gospels of Jesus feeding the vast multitudes with just a couple of fish and a few loaves of bread.

131

Jesus took the offering of a young boy in the crowd, just like you and me—a face in the crowd—and used that offering to feed thousands of people. He will use what we offer to Him for His glory, but we must give Him something to work with. We must live each day in accordance with our priorities, and trust that God will be faithful. God first, others second, self third. This order of precedence will mitigate much of the problem that lies within you and keep you from being a stumbling block for yourself and others. Opposition is unavoidable, but self-conquest and trusting God are the keys to victory.

By the way, the trusting God part is hard. Fear is one of the most popular weapons of the enemy. We often think of temptation as the enticement of something that our sinful human nature desires. There is that pull late at night, when no one is around, to watch some porn; or, when traveling out of town where no one knows your face, when there is no human accountability, to go out, get trashed, and see where the night takes you; the desire to jump on an opportunity to get some extra money in a dishonest way, skimming the books at work, or selling the prescription pills your doctor gave you. These are the things we may think of when it comes to the devil and temptation, but what about the fear that strikes us deep in the soul, paralyzing us, and keeping us from pursuing God's purpose for our lives?

The only way to combat fear is with faith. No amount of rationalization or logical thought can do the trick when it comes to walking in faith. The enemy's objective is, and has always been, to keep us from trusting the loving God who created us. Take a good look at the story of the fall of man in Chapter 3 of Genesis. We can learn a lot about how the enemy works and a great deal about our own sinful human nature. The serpent painted God in a way that did not match His true character: "Did God really say, 'You must not eat from any tree in the garden?'" Then the serpent presents God, not as a loving protector who wants to live in a trusting relationship with man, but instead, a jealous and untrustworthy god who wants to keep people in their place. If we do not trust God, then we fall into the same trap that Eve did and reap the same result: death. What would have happened if Eve had slapped that serpent upside the head with a stick and told Him that God loves her, would never lie to her, and only wants the best for her? It would have changed the entire story. This is the attitude we should have, always. We must trust God. He will deliver us.

Chapter 7
Taste and See That the Lord is Good

As you may suspect, this book has been written for several different purposes. The primary reason that I have written this through the guidance of the Holy Spirit is to share my testimony of God's work in my individual life—to tell you a story about God, through my own personal experience. A secondary purpose is to help those who may have a limited understanding and relationship with God to be elevated to the next level in the Kingdom Life, as a Jesus following, God loving, servant superhero—the type of person who comes off the bench in their Christian walk to transform, redeem, and renew their relationships and communities, to go from lukewarm to hot, to go all in, not just dip their feet in the water but get all the way dripping wet. In the third chapter of the book of Revelation, the resurrected Lord is speaking to certain groups of believers in the early church. To the church in Laodicea came this message, "I know your deeds, that you are neither cold nor hot. I wish you were either one or the other! So, because you are lukewarm—neither hot nor cold—I am about to spit you out of my mouth." (Revelation 3:15-16 NIV)

I also hope to reach other audiences as well, those who have not yet heard, those who are not yet fully convinced, and those who are defiant of the faith. If you don't know Jesus, I am here to hook ya'll up. If you are not a believer, a follower of Christ, a Christian, then this chapter is distinctly directed toward you. In this chapter, I will attempt to say everything that I wish I could have said to The Scientist in our conversation that I mentioned in an earlier chapter. This is my chance to make the argument for Christ with you, a person who I likely will never have the opportunity to meet face to face.

I am not going to pull any punches. This is likely going to upset you to a certain extent. Some may try to reach you by compromising or sugar-coating the truth. To be honest, the message that I am writing here will not be neutral. It will either contribute to your salvation or your condemnation, for in the matter of Jesus, there can be no middle ground. The Lord Himself said, "Whoever is not with me is against me, and whoever does not gather with me scatters." (Matthew 12:30) To us who live in the subjective-morality-driven, post-modern first world culture, this may seem too black and white. But the real Jesus was a polarizing figure without a doubt. You will either be saved or you will be lost. We live in the median currently, where we taste of the fruit of knowledge of good and evil. However, in the end, we will get one or the other, and the time to choose is now.

As I mentioned before, I was listening to a Billy Graham sermon, can't tell you where or when he preached it, but it was a clip from one of his many evangelistic crusades. He always preached for a decision. If we don't decide, then we have made the decision not to decide. Because we are finite, time will eventually make the decision for us in its finality. Rev. Graham presented this scenario, heavily paraphrased by yours truly: say you need to catch a flight to New York City, and there is one leaving your local airport at 7:00 p.m. tomorrow night. That plane is going to roll out whether you are on it or not. You have to decide whether you are going to buy the ticket, drive to the airport, and catch that flight. No matter how much you want to see a play on Broadway or visit the Statue of Liberty, if you don't decide to get on that plane, then it will leave without you.

You may say to yourself, well there are planes to New York all the time, and if I miss that one, I can just jump on the next one. Yeah, but Jesus made it pretty clear that He is the only flight to Heaven, and if you don't have a ticket, you're out of luck. Ya'll know by now that I'm a straight shooter. At a certain time in a certain place in the future, every single one of us is going to die. (Or Jesus is going to come back and take some folks with Him in the Rapture and leave the rest behind, which would be a literal missing your flight scenario—but that is a different discussion.) Regardless, the end shall come for each of us. I find comfort in what Jesus says in John Chapter 14. Jesus is speaking to His disciples about His departure from this world and assuring them that He is preparing a place for them, and at some point in time, He will come back to get them. Thomas, I am sure, represented the rest of the disciples as he was flabbergasted, and probably had no idea what Jesus was talking about when He said, "You know the way to the place where I am going." (14:4) The doubting disciple, Thomas, said, "Lord, we don't know where you are going, so how can we know the way?" (14:5)

That is when Jesus drops the bombshell that immediately confronts everything our modern, secular, and universalist culture tries to stay away from: "I am the way and the truth and the life. **No one** comes to the Father except through me." (14:8) Jesus is claiming to be the exclusive path to Heaven, claiming that the only way for sinful man to reach God is through Him. This directly contradicts the "many different ways to Heaven" perspective that is popular today. People want to label Jesus as a good teacher, and then they can take some of the stuff from His life and ministry—mainly the stuff they like. We can throw those teachings in with other "good teachers," religious figures, and philosophers like Buddha and Socrates, leaving us with a worldview of our own design that clearly displays the hope that we will be alright even if we don't really commit to anything.

It's like betting on sports. Some folks bet a little bit of money on several different games to mitigate their losses and increase their odds of coming out on top. Jesus does not allow us to play that way. He says there is only one game, and you got to place your bet one way or the other. Everybody has their chips in hand, and "all in" is the only acceptable bet. To you, Jesus is God in the flesh, the Messiah, the only way to have forgiveness of sins, the means of atonement. He is the only way to be reconciled to God, the only way to avoid the wrath to come, and the righteous judge of the earth—or He's not. Jesus said, referring to His second coming, **"But when the Son of Man comes in his glory, and all the holy angels**

with him, then he will sit on the throne of his glory. Before him all the nations will be gathered, and he will separate them one from another, as a shepherd separates the sheep from the goats." (Matthew 25:31-33)

There are several different categories of non-believers as I see it. There are those who do not believe that God exists, which makes the whole conversation about Jesus kind of irrelevant because they don't even have a starting point. Then there is the category that I think describes most of the people I know who are not followers of Christ; they believe that God exists but cannot figure out the details enough to make up their minds. Then, of course, there are also those who believe in God but have chosen to follow a different path of worship other than Christianity. In this category are those who practice other faiths and philosophies like Islam and Buddhism. I will attempt in my limited capacity to address each of these groups briefly.

To the Atheist, the anti-theist, and the agnostic, I first would like for you to know that I respect your skepticism. I understand why you might feel the way that you do. There are undoubtedly questions that we do not have adequate answers for in this life. There are so many contradictory worldviews and perceptions of truth, so many counterfeits and con-artists running around, that it is easy to feel like someone is always trying to hustle you. We see so much dishonesty, betrayal, and infidelity in this broken world that it seems naive to think that anything or anybody can be trusted. Whether we like it or not, we are putting our chips on something. Each of us must believe something, even if that belief is in nothing.

For me personally, I cannot possibly believe that all of this came from nothing. I am not a physicist or anything close, but the best I can gather from the Big Bang is that everything started with some sort of massive explosion of a singularity that somehow possessed all the ingredients for the universe, including, but not limited to, life and consciousness. There are laws like gravity that bring order out of chaos and govern the universe, and this requires a lawgiver. Ravi Zacharias once said that thinking the magnificent existence that we see around us and are a part of was to come about by means of the Big Bang would be like thinking that an "encyclopedia was created by an explosion in a printing press." I don't see how it could all just happen. There must have been a first cause, an intelligent being behind the origins of life.

I used to live in the mountains of North Carolina, which are beautiful enough to make a pretty decent case for the existence of the Creator by themselves, truly God's country. Not too far from where we lived was the biggest home in America, the Biltmore estate. If you stood on the front lawn of that massive home, would you say to yourself, "Wow! Isn't it amazing that all this wood, metal, and glass fell from the sky and landed like this?" No, of course not! One would ask the question, "Who built this amazing place?" I got news for you. You are way more amazing than the Biltmore. Your DNA is like a billion-page manual that instructs the body in the way it should develop. On accident? I don't think so.

In the first chapter of Paul's letter to the Romans, the apostle writes, "For since the creation of the world God's invisible qualities—His eternal power and divine nature—have been clearly seen, being understood from what has been made, so that people are without excuse." (Romans 1:20 NIV) When I look at it logically and rationally, the case for the existence of a higher power, a Creator, is clear. In my opinion, God is self-evident, but, as I said before, for many, this is not enough. For God, this is also not enough. Paul also addresses this part of the puzzle; "For although they knew God, they neither glorified him as God nor gave thanks to him, but their thinking became futile and their foolish hearts were darkened. Although they claimed to be wise, they became fools." (Romans 1:21-22 NIV)

God exists; now what? Are all religions fundamentally the same and superficially different? Or, are they superficially similar and different at their core? Do all paths lead to the same mountaintop? As I stated before, Jesus claimed exclusivity as the only way to God. The Son of God spoke often about being the only way to enter into eternal life: "I am the gate; whoever enters through me will be saved." (John 10:9 NIV) With this invitation comes a warning about refusal to RSVP, Jesus' full disclosure statement from a different gospel: "Enter through the narrow gate. For wide is the gate and broad is the road that leads to destruction, and many enter through it. But small is the gate and narrow the road that leads to life, and only a few find it." (Matthew 7:13-14 NIV)

So if it is as simple as a decision then why do so few find it? Well, because this decision is conditional. What are the conditions? You have to go all in. "Jesus said to his disciples, "Whoever wants to be my disciple must deny themselves and take up their cross and follow me." It requires sacrifice. I must turn from my sinful and self-centered way of living to be focused solely on living for God and following the example of Christ. Though some may be asked to die for their faith in Christ, all are called to live for Him. "For whoever wants to save their life will lose it, but whoever loses their life for me will find it." (Matthew 16:24-25 NIV) This is why so many people say that they gave their lives to Christ. For the Christian, the real Jesus-loving ones, the old them is gone, and they are a new creation in Christ Jesus, living solely for Him. It is not just going to church on Sunday and putting some money in the plate; it is so much more than that.

But why should I give my life to Christ? Prove it. You want me to bet all my chips on some illegitimate child of a handyman and a teenage Jewish girl, in some place that probably doesn't even exist anymore, who taught 2000 years ago, and got killed because He got too popular as a rabbi in Israel while the Romans were in town? Yep. Why? Mainly, because he came back from the dead. Sure, there are a ton of other good answers that I can put in there, like prophecies fulfilled, blind people seeing stuff, dead folks coming back brand new like they woke up from a siesta, and telling storms to shut up and sit down. My favorite evidence is the resurrection of Jesus on the third day. Jesus coming back from the dead is the game changer and separates Him from any other. Why do I believe that the resurrection actually happened? Street smarts.

Jesus picked up a bunch of regular dudes off the street to be His disciples. If His followers were religious leaders and politicians, I would be super skeptical, because they would have the power to make up some bogus story and keep it going. Each of these regular dudes was visibly changed by something that went down in Jerusalem. Their true colors showed in the Garden when Jesus got arrested. Mark 14:50 puts it this way: "Then everyone deserted Him and ran away." Sure, Peter put up some fight with a sword, but then it was every man for himself. Who could blame them? The jig was up, they had the leader in chains; *Time to cut ties and save yourselves!* It's just like when you are on the corner doing nefarious things and the cops roll up, poof, and everyone scatters like roaches. Whoever gets caught with the stuff is in for it, and they better not snitch. Their attitude was similar: "We had a good run with the Miracle Man, but it doesn't look good for Him; I guess we'll head back to Galilee and start fishing again."

Then, as they are hiding and sulking, licking their wounds, and trying to figure out what to do next, some of Jesus' homegirls roll in, talking about how His body is missing, and they don't know where He is.—which does not line up with a conspiracy theory because women's testimonies were not considered valid back in those days. Having women be the first to report the resurrection would point to the fact that it really happened, instead of it being a deceptive plot. If you were going to fake it, then you would not use women as the first eyewitnesses to the resurrected Christ. Next, Jesus appears to all of the disciples and a lot of other folks over the period of forty days between His resurrection and ascension. A tremendous transformation takes place.

After witnessing the resurrected Christ, all of his followers, who were the run-and-hide type, were ready and willing to die for their eyewitness testimony of this truth. In fact, most of them did die for the faith, and not only that, they got roughed up pretty often:

whipped, imprisoned, had their possessions taken away, poisoned, and lots of other interesting brutalities. That is a pretty dramatic transition from turning and running in the garden or hiding out in the Upper Room with the door bolted shut for fear that they would be discovered. I know what you're thinking, *but Muslim extremists die for what they believe in all the time, so how is this any different?* The Muslim extremists believe that their faith is true, but they do not know for sure whether it is or isn't. These guys, on the other hand, knew if what they believed was true or not. Either they chose to die to share their eyewitness testimonies of the Resurrection or they chose to die to prolong a narrative they knew was made up.

As I mentioned before, these were regular dudes off the streets, fishermen and day laborers. Sure, someone may die for something that they think is true, but ain't nobody going to die for something that they know is not true. If Jesus really did not rise from the dead, then the disciples surely would have known that. Can you picture Peter and John sitting in prison with lashes in their back, saying, "Oh man, this whole lying about Jesus coming back from the dead thing is really working out! We gotta keep this rolling. Oh yeah! John, I heard your brother James got his head chopped off the other day. Sweet! We got 'em right where we want 'em now!" To be honest, being a first century Christian sucked! Why would anyone go through that for something they knew was a lie?

When I take a good hard look at the evidence, it becomes clear to me that Jesus really did get crucified, die on the Cross, and come back to life. Try to find someone else who did that supported by real evidence. In John Chapter 10, Jesus says something that is pretty striking: "No one can take my life from me. I sacrifice it voluntarily. For I have the authority to lay it down when I want to and also to take it up again." (NLT) Surely someone who has the ability to raise himself from the dead can keep himself from getting killed in the first place, right? No doubt. So why did He do it? He did it for me. He did it for you. He thinks that you're worth dying for.

As Isaiah 1:18 says, "Come let us reason together." Do people do bad things? Yes. Do people who do bad things deserve to be punished for the wrongs they have done? Without a doubt. A righteous and Holy God would be unjust if He did not punish the wrongs that have been committed. We cry out when injustice happens in our own courts of law. We shake our heads as someone gets a lenient sentence because of their money or influence. When someone is acquitted of a horrible crime because of a technicality or someone is granted bond who clearly should be kept behind bars, these things enrage us. The only problem is that each of us is guilty before a Holy and righteous God, some worse than others, but all are guilty. Each of us deserves what's coming to us, whether we like it or not, but what if the Judge says, "Would you be interested in a pardon?"

Who would not jump on that offer, right? What do I need to do? The judge says, " I will take your punishment for you, because the price has to be paid. In exchange, your life now belongs to me. You will be my child, a member of my family and my kingdom, forever. You will no longer do things your way but will live a completely different life. I will help you and give you everything you need to do it. Do you accept my offer?" Well, do you?

If you have decided to accept this offer, in the next chapter I will give you a basic run down of what happens next. It will serve as a guideline, as I see it, to beginning and sustaining your new life with Christ. If you are not convinced after reading the evidence that is laid out before you in this chapter and all of the previous material with regards to all that God has done in my life, then I say to you, missing this flight will be the absolute worst decision you have ever made. My friend, though you may see yourself as a relatively "good" person, each of us stands condemned before a Holy God whose wrath is more than we can bear.

"Since we have now been justified by His blood, how much more shall we be saved from God's wrath through Him! For if, while we

were God's enemies, we were reconciled to Him through the death of His Son, how much more, having been reconciled, shall we be saved through His life!" (Romans 5:9-10)

Chapter 8
Behold I am Making All Things New

First and foremost, I think that it is important that I state that I am against "flu-shot Christianity." This, as I perceive it, is one of the most dangerous concepts of faith in America. Flu-shot Christianity is when you say a prayer, and then poof, you magically get to go to Heaven when you die, even though there is no real change, and you live exactly like you always did before. It's like getting an immunization so you don't contract eternal damnation. I've heard Paul Washer preach about this many times and lay out a pretty good way to spot the symptoms of this type of superficial faith. Say you ask someone if they are a Christian, they may respond with, "Yeah I said that prayer one time, I'm good."

I was a flu-shot Christian at best before I really started my relationship with Christ. Don't get me wrong, it does start with a prayer, but that is not the end; it is only the beginning. The point is, don't just say a prayer and then think that everything is all fine and dandy, that you can do whatever you want, and everything will be okay just because you said the sinner's prayer. To think such a thing is a great insult to God, the sacrifice of Christ, and the real Christians who have given everything for their faith.

You are not just checking the box; you are swearing allegiance and eternal servitude to the King of kings and the Lord of lords who came in human flesh and died so that you could live eternally. However, you are doing this because you realize that God loves you even more than you love yourself, that He knows what is best for you, and He will lead you to true joy and fulfillment as you walk with Him. You are making Jesus the end-all and be-all focal point of your life. In Matthew's Gospel, the Lord speaks about making Him the foundation of our life: "Therefore everyone who hears these words of mine and puts them into practice is like a wise man who built his house on the rock. The rain came down, the

144

streams rose, and the winds blew and beat against that house; yet it did not fall, because it had its foundation on the rock. But everyone who hears these words of mine and does not put them into practice is like a foolish man who built his house on sand. The rain came down, the streams rose, and the winds blew and beat against that house, and it fell with a great crash." (7:24-27 NIV) If you are a young person who is reading this book and have yet to really begin to "build your house," then it is my advice to let your life be built upon the rock of the Lord. Just give it all to Jesus now because He will guide you on a path that not only leads to Heaven, but also to an abundant, happy, and fulfilled life on Earth. For those of you who are older and have already "built your house" on the values of this world, well, there is no easy way to say this; you're going to have to tear your house down and rebuild on a new foundation, figuratively speaking. But God will help you do this. He will change the desires of your heart to things that lead to blessings for you and others. This is a process known as sanctification.

When I first got to basic training at Fort Sill, Oklahoma I was a cocky "wanna be" thug. I knew everything, and you couldn't tell me nothing. But the Army has designed basic training with the objective of tearing you down so that they can build you back up again. Brother, let me tell ya, it works. After that seventeen weeks of Basic and Advanced Individual Training. I was a different person in many ways.

The Christian life is a lot like that. There are some things that will need to go. I can remember when I was a kid, my dad brought home this thing that moderately resembled some type of vehicle. It was just a naked chassis that apparently had previously belonged to a Camaro, if I am not mistaken. I have a picture of the first time it appeared in our driveway. Just for kicks, my dad had attached a steering wheel and set a bucket seat on the driver's side for the photo. It was quite comedic actually.

I did not have the vision to see it, but he said that the goal was to build it into a 1957 Chevy hotrod truck. It took a long time, lots of money, and multiple trips back to the drawing board. He had to find subject matter experts in all of the areas where he lacked knowledge and experience, but one day his dream became a reality. To see the finished product, you could never have possibly guessed how it started. An old rusted out Camaro had to be torn down to the bare chassis, in order to be built into one of the most beautiful machines I have ever seen. It was a process that surely was not completed overnight. But it was started instantly.

You have been given a fresh start. If you will work with Him, then God, through the power of the Holy Spirit, will turn you into a super-dope dream ride, figuratively speaking. Check out what the Apostle Paul says to the church in Corinth; "He died for everyone so that those who receive His new life will no longer live for themselves. Instead, they will live for Christ who has died and was raised for them. This means that anyone who belongs to Christ has become a new person. The old life is gone; a new life has begun!" (2 Corinthians 5:15, 17 NLT)

People can be justified instantly at the decision to give their lives to Christ in faith, depending on Him for the forgiveness of their sins. Romans 10:9-10 says, "If you declare with your mouth 'Jesus is Lord,' and believe in your heart that God has raised Him from the dead, you will be saved. For it is with your heart that you believe and are justified, and it is with your mouth that you profess your faith and are saved." (NIV) But like I mentioned before, this is not the end; it is only the beginning.

Remember that the devil has two primary objectives. The first is to keep you from your own personal salvation and reconciliation with God. He wants us to die in our sins, so that we can burn in Hell like he is going to. Satan is already condemned, and his end is certain, so he is looking to take as many people with him as possible. Misery loves company. So, now that he has failed in his first objective, it is now onto his secondary mission of causing you to be fruitless and ineffective in your ministry to others. It is his desire to kill your witness and to make you the worst possible follower of Christ you can be. This can be done in many subtle ways. Perhaps, it is to keep you so comfortable that you don't pray and seek God. Or, perhaps it is to constantly bring to your mind sins that have been forgiven by God but make you feel like you're not good enough so you never reach your true, grace-filled potential as a redeemed child of God. Or, maybe it is the same trick he has always used, trying to get you to bite that apple of temptation, have that affair, cook those books, or tell that little lie to get ahead. How many people have walked out on God, quit the church, turned their back on Jesus, because of something that a Christian did?

How many people want nothing to do with the faith because of greedy, money swindling pastors whose double lives have been exposed? How many are ashamed to speak the name of Jesus for fear that they will be thrown in with the likes of child-molesting priests or hypocritical church leaders who bash homosexuals and other folks who sin differently than they do, and then cheat on their wives with their secretaries? You know it's true.

You have been given a fresh start, try not to mess it up.

I feel so ashamed for all the times that I have made Jesus look bad. As a professing Christian, we are the representatives of Jesus in this world. Just as the twelve Apostles turned the world upside down as His witnesses, we are called to the same tremendous task to the ends of the earth. We must be fully aware that in this calling, Jesus will be judged through our actions. Your life is the only Bible some folks will ever read.

This is why it is so important that you go all in with the Christian life. You will be a work in progress until the day that you go to be glorified with the Lord. It is a war. I am still fighting much of the old me. Have I won many battles? Yes, without a doubt. Have I conquered the flesh in many areas? Sure. Am I done yet? Nope, not by a long shot. I still have habits that need to be destroyed. From time to time, dark spots that I thought I had beat long ago will pop up and rear their ugly heads. It is war. I can remember hearing a preacher one time who said, "When is it gonna get easier? When you die!" That's a little dramatic, but really, nothing that we go through here on earth can compare to what waits for those who love the Lord. By the way, I highly recommend the book by Levi Lusko, *I Declare War,* for more insight on the battles of the Christian life.

You should seek out spiritual mentors wherever you can, and the only way you can tell if they are real or frauds is by studying the Bible. I have a list of spiritual influencers that have helped me continually refocus my mind on the Lord. We live in an age where we can access unlimited hours of great preaching and teaching from passionate leaders in the faith like Paul Washer and Francis Chan. I listen to podcasts of sermons daily, some of my favorites are *Summit Life* with J.D. Greear and *The Encouraging Word* with Dr. Don Wilton. Read some great books. Trust me, nobody hated reading more than this guy! But do it anyway. I have been reading a daily devotional entitled *God Calling* since before the mission trip, and I still find it very enriching. I was also deeply blessed by reading the Billy Graham Biography *Just As I Am.* Seek. Keep seeking. "Ask, and it will be given to you; seek, and you will find; knock, and the door will be opened to you." (Matthew 7:7)

You will also need to be a part of a body of believers, the local church, and the greater Church as a whole. Find one that works or start your own. I don't know what God has planned specifically for you, but I do know that having fellowship with others who are part of the body of Christ is a necessity. Find mentors, people who already are where you want to be in their lives. Learn from them. I have several of these. Look to them for guidance, wisdom, advice, and accountability. Surround yourself with people who absolutely love Jesus, and you will be continually blessed and prayed for along your journey.

This next part is the hardest thing that you will need to do, but I hope that you will. If you have come to the foot of the Cross to receive the forgiveness that Jesus paid so great a price to purchase, you must now give that forgiveness to others. I can distinctly remember when this verse jumped off the page and sank deep into my heart; "But if you do not forgive others their sins, your Father will not forgive your sins." (Matthew 6:15) There was a night when I was alone in the basement with God. During this time, I poured out my heart to God and brought to memory everything that I knew I had done wrong. I asked forgiveness for every sin I had committed that I could remember and prayed for the people affected by my actions. Then I went through the painful task of forgiving everyone who hurt or harmed me: the bullies, the girls who had wounded me with their infidelities, my dad, friends who betrayed me, the guys who blew me up, everybody.

I realize to some extent how painful this will be and has been for you. I realize what it means. How can I forgive that person? The frat boy who raped you when you had a little too much to drink, the drunk driver who killed your child, the step-dad who used to come into your bedroom late at night, the drug dealer who sold the stuff your son overdosed on, the dad who abandoned you and your family, the affair, the business partner who robbed you blind. Jesus died for them too. I know it feels like forgiving someone is just letting them off the hook. Remember, vengeance belongs to the Lord. He will sort it out. These sins will either lead to their salvation and transformation into a better person, as they did with me, or their eternal condemnation and punishment. Either way, God is the judge, not us. Let God have it, otherwise, it will continue to poison your soul. "But I tell you, love your enemies and pray for those who persecute you, that you may be children of your Father in heaven." (Matthew 5:44,45)

There is something beautiful that happens when we truly forgive and realize the forgiveness we have received from God. We have a peace that is unlike any other. It also opens the doors for renewed relationships and new beginnings. For instance, after a very rocky relationship for most of my life, my dad and I have become very close in recent years. Now, I not only consider him my dad, but also a dear friend. I see this as something only God could have worked out. "We love because He first loved us." (1 John 4:19)

149

Continued from the second letter to the Corinthians, Paul writes, "All of this is a gift from God, who brought us back to himself through Christ. And God has given us this task of reconciling people to Him. For God was in Christ reconciling the world to himself, no longer counting people's sins against them. And He gave us this wonderful message of reconciliation. So we are Christ's ambassadors; God is making his appeal through us. We speak for Christ when we plead, 'Come back to God!' For God made Christ who never sinned to be the offering for our sin, so that we could be made right with God through Christ." (2 Corinthians 5:18-21 NLT)

Jesus died for you. Now your Lord has assigned you with the mission of saving the world. You are commanded to love God and love people. What are you going to do about it? I'm all in!

If you are moved by this story, I ask that you support these causes close to my heart:

Operation Heal Our Patriots
My wife and I participated in this program that helps to heal and restore the marriages of wounded veterans and their spouses in the name of Jesus. It was a game changer for us! I, along with many others, have been baptized in those cold Alaskan waters. Learn more at: https://www.samaritanspurse.org/what-we-do/about-operation-heal-our-patriots/

Life Decisions
This is a program that focuses on providing solutions for the full spectrum of challenges that face at-risk, high-risk, and Juvenile Justice affected youth. I am honored to partner with Life Decisions. Please check us out at: https://www.lifedecisions.net/

Stateline Youth for Christ
I am honored to also work with this organization that cares so deeply for our young people. I believe that Jesus changes people, and then those people change the world around them. See how this happens at: https://www.statelineyfc.org/

CPSIA information can be obtained
at www.ICGtesting.com
Printed in the USA
LVHW011149080721
691987LV00012B/507